Developing Critical Thinking

The Speaking/Listening Connection

Developing Critical Thinking

The Speaking/Listening Connection

Virginia O'Keefe

Boynton/Cook Publishers Inc.
HEINEMANN
Portsmouth, NH

Boynton/Cook Publishers, Inc.
A subsidiary of Reed Elsevier Inc.
361 Hanover Street
Portsmouth, NH 03801–3912
www.boyntoncook.com

Offices and agents throughout the world

The author and publisher wish to thank those who have generously given permission to reprint borrowed material:

"Shyness Scale" from *Quiet Children and the Classroom Teacher, 2nd Edition* by James C. McCroskey and Virginia P. Richmond. Copyright © 1991. Originally published by ERIC and Speech Communication Association. Reprinted by permission of the National Communication Association.

Appendix A: From *Standards for the English Language Arts* by the International Reading Association and the National Council of Teachers of English. Copyright © 1996 by the National Council of Teachers of English. Originally published by the International Reading Association and the National Council of Teachers of English. Reprinted by permission.

Appendix B: From *Competent Communications K–12: Speaking, Listening, and Media Literacy Standards and Competency Statements* by Speech Communication Association. Copyright © 1998 by the National Communication Association. Reprinted by permission.

Appendix C: From *The National Curriculum* (http://www.dfee.gov.uk/nc/engk3html). Reprinted by permission of the Controller of Her Majesty's Stationery Office.

Library of Congress Cataloging-in-Publication Data
O'Keefe, Virginia P.
    Developing critical thinking : the speaking/listening connection / Virginia O'Keefe.
    p. cm.
    Includes bibliographical references and index.
    ISBN 0-86709-491-5
    1. Oral communication—Study and teaching. 2. Critical thinking. I. Title.
    P91.3.034 1999
    302.2'242' 07—dc21   99-30811
                                                     CIP

Editor: Lisa Luedeke
Production: Elizabeth Valway
Cover design: Joni Doherty Design
Manufacturing: Louise Richardson

Printed in the United States of America on acid-free paper
03 02 01 00 99 DA 1 2 3 4 5

Contents

Foreword

Throughout the country, a serious misperception affects English teachers and their instruction. English teachers are supposed to be teaching the "language arts," but they restrict their efforts to a concentration on reading and writing skills. I can understand why they do this, of course. How many stories have we seen in the popular media exploring the issue of "Why Johnny Can't *Write* [or *Read*]"? The articles and stories we see on these subjects are rarely concerned with students' communication skills in general. Instead, the stories—and the nation—remain focused on reading and writing skills. Students' reading and writing abilities are tested and monitored constantly, and exam scores are publicized everywhere, often accompanied by complaints about the dismal results and calls for renewed emphasis on these particular aspects of the curriculum.

Teachers' preparation at universities and colleges, moreover, often consists of an extensive study of literature and literary instruction and, perhaps, the completion of several rhetoric and writing courses. No wonder, then, that English teachers have come to see themselves as teachers of reading and writing.

This distorted view of the language arts—this misperception—prevents teachers from understanding the importance of what Virginia O'Keefe calls the *Speaking/Listening Connection*. Oral communication is the primary means through which instruction in almost all disciplines is accomplished—for instance, students ask questions and seek clarification and elaboration of assignments and directions, all through speaking and listening. Increasingly, recommended instructional practices call for students to construct, negotiate, and communicate meanings through their own classroom talk, and revise and edit their writing in small groups.

It makes sense, then, to focus on students' speaking and listening skills and incorporate them into our lessons and activities. Virginia O'Keefe possesses this insight and shows in her book how to accomplish this important task. She describes and demonstrates many valuable ways to use students' own talk as a vehicle for learning, expands our repertoire of instructional options for developing students' speaking and listening abilities, shows us how to truly engage students in effective and worthwhile meaning-making activities, and convinces us of the centrality of oral communication in every classroom and every instructional design.

Virginia's instructional approach also clears up another misperception that pervades our schools and curricula. I have observed several schools that list among their course offerings a separate class for "Critical Thinking." This is problematic for a couple of reasons: the assumptions behind this practice appear to be that one can *teach* critical thinking directly and that one can develop students' critical thinking skills in isolation from other subjects and disciplines.

But Virginia sees the fallacies inherent in this practice and corrects the problem through her arguments and activities in this volume. She realizes that one does not *teach* critical thinking; instead, one designs and structures classroom activities in such a way that *critical thinking happens*. As students participate in these activities requiring the exercise of the various critical thinking skills, they are coached and directed by the teacher to articulate and elaborate on their thinking processes. In this way, students' critical thinking skills are *affected* and made "new and improved."

There are lessons to be learned here: about the use of students' own talk as a vehicle for learning; about ways to enable students to participate actively in their own education; and about what's worth knowing and doing in the classroom.

It is unfortunate that too few teachers understand the speaking/ listening connection and its role in making learning happen for students. Happily, with the publication of this book, there will soon be more who do.

Jeffrey N. Golub
Associate Professor of English Education
University of South Florida, Tampa

Acknowledgments

The ideas and much of the information in *Developing Critical Thinking: The Speaking/Listening Connection* first appeared in *Affecting Critical Thinking through Speech*, published by the Speech Communication Association, now the National Communication Association (NCA), and the ERIC Clearinghouse on Reading and Communication Skills Office of Educational Research and Improvement. Although more than a decade has passed since then, the situation in secondary language arts instruction is much the same. Speaking and listening skills receive less attention in the classroom than reading and writing. The premise of this book is that a communication-based environment promotes better thinking. If students experience learning in ways that encourage talking and listening, dramatic performance, small group participation, and creative response, they have a chance to increase their repertoire of communication skills. When they form ideas, test meanings, receive feedback, and interact in a social setting, they also tap their own innate abilities to think more effectively.

The theory, guidelines, and detailed instructions aid teachers who want to place more emphasis on speaking and listening skills. Activities are classroom tested; therefore, while theoretically sound, they also provide a practical approach for teachers who wish to incorporate oral communication into a language arts setting.

I wish to thank the members and officers of the National Communication Association for their support of the original project and their scholarly advice. I especially thank Don Boileau, who encouraged me to share these ideas with educators across the curriculum. I also wish to thank Lisa Luedeke, who encouraged me to expand the original book into this updated and more comprehensive resource for teachers.

One

Critical Thinking
in the Classroom

Speaking and listening have two important functions. The first is interpersonal, or relational, allowing us to communicate with others. The second is intrapersonal, or ideational, allowing us to communicate with ourselves. Thus, the teaching of language is also the teaching of thinking, and this book is primarily concerned with that aspect of speaking and listening. As educators, we have become increasingly aware of the value of writing in the learning process. We have been less cognizant of the need to talk out ideas as a key ingredient of comprehension. In general, we have assumed that hearing is the same as listening and have treated speaking as though it were transparent, something done to achieve a product.

After years of experience in the classroom, from elementary grades through high school, I am convinced that students are consistently shortchanged. The problem lies with how our preconceived ideas about thinking and intelligence work against most youngsters. From K–12, students often reach us in presorted sets. Set A are the bright children, the ones to whom we give the most exciting assignments. Set B are the average, who get a mixture of the routine and the novel. For Set C, the "at-risks," all of the challenges belong to the teacher.

As we enter the twenty-first century, the picture appears to be getting darker. More students, rather than less, are categorized as school failures. A school superintendent in Virginia says that hundreds and hundreds of his district's students will be failing high school when the state institutes its new standards requirement. Are students really so deficient? I think not. Evidence from research and classroom practice indicates that except for rare instances, everyone is born with an ability

1

to think (Smith 1990). Our job is to tap youngsters' natural talent for thinking and inborn capacity to make sense of the world. The purpose of this book is to provide connections between speech and thought that mirror what happens in our everyday lives.

The first chapter discusses the theoretical and research background for using speaking and listening to affect critical thinking. The second chapter explains the structure and dynamics of the communication-based classroom. Chapter 3 explores three thinking skills: reasoning, predicting, and projecting, along with activities for developing each skill.

The Need for Critical Thinking

I am certain that many teachers share my optimism about the potential for learning in our schools. However, the other side of the story is reported daily: how teachers don't motivate, how students don't learn to think. We read about dismal SAT scores. The Third International Math and Science Study (TIMSS) made headlines when U.S. students fell below, or close to average, in comparison with twenty-one other countries (Hiraoka 1998, 19).

Schools' inferior results have been faulted for decades. Benjamin Bloom found that of the six classes of learning, the "lowest," *knowledge,* or acquisition of facts, was the most common objective in American education (1979, 28). He called for schools to provide more experience in the complex and higher categories of cognition. Students should be allowed to participate more actively in the learning process.

In the 1980s, criticism of public education mounted. Mortimer Adler (1982) found our schools in deplorable condition. Ernest Boyer (1983) gave the schools a mixed report card, claiming only the top 10 to 15 percent of students received an outstanding education. These youngsters were challenged to think creatively and critically, as well as to remember and respond. The other 60 percent of students who got anything at all out of high school, Boyer claimed, received little intellectual challenge. The sharpest attack came from the National Commission on Excellence in Education, which declared in the now famous *A Nation at Risk,* that our mediocre educational system placed us at jeopardy in the world (McClellan 1994).

That last report triggered a mood for national educational reform, and in February 1990, President Bush, along with the state governors, established six national education goals to be met by the year 2000. These goals were signed into law during President Clinton's administration.

While not establishing a national curriculum, the goals have inspired educators and policy makers to focus on what learners should master if they are to function well in our complex society. Goal Three, for example, states that students will leave grades 4, 8, and 12 with competency in challenging subject matter, and that they will be prepared, upon high school graduation, for responsible citizenship, further learning, and productive employment ("Meeting Goal 3: How Well Are We Doing?" 1992, 1). Almost ten years have passed since these goals were instituted, and we can examine the record to learn how well they have been met.

Some progress has been made. We have an all-time high rate for secondary school graduations, with 86 percent of twenty-one-to twenty-two-year-olds completing high school, when we include delayed graduations and GED figures. Approximately 60 percent of U.S. high school graduates go on to postsecondary schools (Freeman 1995). One in four American adults receives bachelor's degrees, the largest percentage for industrialized countries ("Within Reach?" 1998). More students than ever, from more schools, are taking Advanced Placement tests and receiving the passing score of 3.02. Six hundred and thirty-five thousand students qualified for credit or placement into advanced courses at colleges and universities ("Average Score on AP Tests High Enough to Earn Credits, Placement" 1996). This past decade has seen the number of students taking core academic courses rise by 27 percent, and the percentage is still going up (Riley 1995). These statistics reveal that American students are not lacking in the brains department.

On the other hand, recent reports from National Assessment of Education Progress (NAEP) indicate that while most students master basic skills, only a small percentage can synthesize data from a variety of reading materials. Less than half of seventeen-year-olds can find, understand, summarize, and explain complicated material in a text (Patrick 1993).

Disappointing test scores can be explained in a number of ways. Students stay in school longer than a generation ago. Those who would have been dropouts in the "good old days" are still sitting in their seats, taking tests, and lowering averages. More take Advanced Placement and SAT tests. In some school districts, seventh- and eighth-grade students are taking the SATs to improve their test-taking savvy. Instead of criticizing low SAT scores, we should commend our schools for helping such a broad population to score as well as they do. We teach math and science courses on different schedules than do our foreign counterparts, and our youngsters may be competing with much older students. In short, despite newspaper accounts to the contrary, American schools are doing quite well by our youth. Nevertheless, the demands of an increasingly complex world require even more sophisticated skills.

David Perkins (1992) in *Smart Schools* labels the two greatest schooling faults as *fragile knowledge,* when students do not remember or understand information, and *poor thinking,* when students cannot think well about what they do know. The cause for this gap is at least partially explained by two ideas in American education. The first is the belief that accumulating facts equates with learning. If we question the popularity of that position, witness the demand for multiple-choice tests to measure achievement. The second is equally pervasive. We hold that ability counts more than effort, and, even more debilitating, that ability is a fixed property. Due to this conviction, youngsters are grouped in ever earlier grades and receive different treatments, accordingly.

Standards

To address the perceived education shortfall, the public demanded accountability. Educational organizations set to work developing national standards for their disciplines. Of the many kinds of standards that can be devised, two are most popular: *performance standards,* which describe through tasks what students should know and do, and *content standards,* which focus on what students should know and be able to do within a subject area.

Controversy over what national standards should contain, and the fear of federal control, led individual states to set standards of their own. Invariably, these standards require higher-order thinking. For example, the *Standards of Learning for Virginia Public Schools* expect students in ninth-grade English to "synthesize information from sources and apply it in written and oral presentations" (1995, 72). Likewise, the *Arkansas English Language Arts and Mathematics Curriculum Frameworks* expect students in grades 5 through 8 to "analyze related and implied main ideas and supportive details" (1993, 5). Both of these documents refer to Bloom's (1979) categories for higher-level cognition, *synthesis* and *analysis*.

In addition to a higher level of thinking, an important feature of English standards is the expanded notion of literacy. Communication, language arts, and reading education organizations include speaking and listening as part of their standards for language competency. The National Council of Teachers of English (NCTE) and the International Reading Association (IRA) refer to spoken language in *Standards for the English Language Arts* (1996), and the NCTE companion book, *Standards in Practice Grades 9–12* (Smagorinsky 1996), contains many examples of oral communication. The National Communication Association (NCA), formerly the Speech Communication Association, with contributions from the International Listening Association (ILA), developed *Competent Communicators* (1998), a document that outlines standards for listening and speaking with their corresponding competencies.

Most state standards also include listening and speaking, usually under English language arts. Approaches differ, however. Some states view speaking, listening, reading, and writing as inseparable processes. The North Carolina *Teacher Handbook Communication Skills K–12* (1992), for one, emphasizes the importance of all forms of language. Students are expected to use effective response skills as they comprehend or convey information and experiences. Other states, such as New York (*Framework for English Language Arts* 1994), pair listening with reading standards, and speaking with writing standards, emphasizing similar requirements for both modes. A very few states list separate standards and objectives for speaking and listening (Hall, Morreale, and Gaudino 1999). All of the states envision that higher standards for speaking and listening will correspondingly raise levels of comprehension and expression.

American teachers are not alone in this race for greater literacy. In Canada, many students are found to lack basic literacy and numeracy skills, evidenced by high failure and dropout rates, as much as 50 percent in some areas of Montreal (*Research Overview* 1998). The United Kingdom (U.K.) has encountered similar gaps between expectations and achievement. Both Canada and the U.K. have instituted national programs to improve performance. Teachers on both sides of the Atlantic are faced with the daunting problem of designing instructional programs that will attain high literacy standards for *all* students, regardless of ability or language background. We can appreciate the difficulty of this task when we realize that no society in the history of the world has ever achieved high literacy rates for a total population.

To assist in instructional planning, therefore, standards for oral communication based on the NCTE, NCA, and U.K. standards are described in Chapter 2. In Chapter 3, selected standards are matched with exercises. (See the NCTE, NCA, and U.K. standards in the Appendices.)

Assessment

In the wake of establishing standards, policy makers and educators struggle to devise instruments that measure whether, and how well, goals are being met. Ironically, the most popular form of assessment, the multiple-choice standardized test, is the least likely to foster better thinking. These tests favor lower-order thought, memorization and recall, and fail to link into the process of learning. They are geared to what David Perkins calls a "Trivial Pursuit" (1992, 20) theory of learning, the mere accumulation of facts and routines.

A more reliable and beneficial method is to use *embedded assessment*, evaluations that are integral to the whole of instruction (O'Keefe 1995). We can visualize these assessments as ongoing feedback, continually informing both the student and teacher about what works well and what needs improvement. The measures, goals, and delivery differ with each assignment. Instead of focusing on ability and a pass/fail mark, embedded assessments place more emphasis on effort. They foster higher-order thinking, supported by an atmosphere where it is OK to make mistakes; it is OK to experiment. Furthermore, as students share in the process, they "own" the assessments as aids to self-improvement. They set goals and measure their progress, much as an athlete or competitive speaker does. Using assessments to gauge improvement, not just to mark the final result, is especially compatible with problem-solving assignments and small group work.

Embedded assessments support the theory that students learn best when they are guided toward meaningful thinking. At times, teachers will leave the comfort zone at the front of the room and play the role of coach on the side. When products are evaluated, their measurements include process. The teacher does not make all of the assessments. Students devise some. They use self-checks. Peers coach, advise, and teach. Journal writings reflect on learning.

As worthwhile as embedded assessments are, they present problems. They tend to be more qualitative than quantitative. Narrative comments are perceived as less objective, and, thus, less valuable than letter grades. Policy makers pressure for accountability, as though numbers on portfolios are more valid than dialogues with students about progress. Parents and students want traditional grades. Fortunately, these desires for so-called objectivity are not necessarily incompatible with embedded assessment. The criteria for grades can be established according to the goals of learning. Feedback in various forms can accompany the numbers, and Chapter 3 suggests a variety of embedded assessments as part of the activities.

The Thinking Curriculum

Our subject matter in and by itself does not produce better thinking. Great lectures, interesting literature, study questions, and demanding curricula are not enough to evoke strong thinking. Students must be invited to think and, then, guided in the process. As teachers, we have to encourage all students, not just the elite, to move beyond rote memorization and recall into more analytical and probing thinking skills. To answer this need, experts and textbook firms suggest various cure-alls: courses in logic, prepared materials, and computer programs. Such "solutions" often treat critical thinking as a separate entity, rather than something that should be integrated with the existing curriculum. On the other hand, programs that recommend infusing specific thinking skills into existing lessons can make the effort so difficult they are unsustainable. One such program suggests that the teacher keep numerical scores on no less than thirteen separate thinking skills (Marzano, Pickering, and McTighe 1993, 37).

Theoretically, keeping records of students' progress on types of thinking skills may appear sound. How else would we know that higher-order thinking is taking place? Unfortunately, even experts cannot agree on the thinking categories that take place during any given event. All too often, this kind of "thinking" program leads to playing a numbers game and serves to stifle thought more than promote it. More damaging, the labeling becomes just another way to fit children into little boxes.

It makes more sense to adopt a holistic approach to thinking, remembering that the processes are neither linear nor hierarchical, and that we can foster better thinking by altering the *way* we teach our present content courses. We can do this without introducing another topic into an already crowded schedule. Nor do we have to pigeonhole every discrete kind of thinking in order to foster these skills. In reality, analysis and synthesis, for example, are inseparable. Analytic thought focuses on detail, but the details are always related to a whole.

Critical thinking is not a subject but a means to achieve a result. Therefore, learning to value thinking, and how the process of speaking and listening affects it, may involve a shift of mental gears—for both the teacher and the students. While it may save time if the teacher dictates facts and students memorize them, more lasting learning takes place if students discover answers with the teacher's guidance. Sometimes the answers will be different from what the teacher expected. Sometimes the answers will be wrong. But becoming an authentic critical thinker involves taking risks, asking questions, and readjusting previous beliefs. An effective program involves both teacher and students in that process.

Brain Studies

Although the research is quite young and many mysteries remain, the brain is no longer quite the "black box" it once was. With compelling evidence from "brain scanners," neuroscientists have been able to watch the brains of living subjects in action. What they have found has implications for teaching. Scientists have seen the kinds of experiences that stimulate the brain and how various parts of the brain work together.

Some new findings contradict previous assumptions. Ideas about "right" brain and "left" brain are outdated. For example, experienced musicians process music in their left hemisphere and expert problem solvers use the right hemisphere (Jensen 1998, 77). And, most significant of all, we have learned that the brain has *plasticity* and *flexibility,* allowing it to continually change and, even more surprisingly, to grow. The brain "rewires" itself with each new stimulation. Learning brings about physical change, and throughout our lives, we can get smarter if we grow more synaptic connections between brain cells.

The brain's potential is not fixed. The more complex connections we develop, the better able we are to figure things out. As adults, our brains have one hundred billion neurons, the cells that make the brain think and learn, and each neuron has several thousand synapses. The brain is a virtual universe of possibilities and is enriched by encountering complex problems. Interestingly enough, research shows that neural growth occurs as a response to working on a problem, regardless of whether a solution is found or not. These brain studies support the earlier education theorists who believed children should be challenged by a more problem-solving environment.

Now, consider how schools traditionally treat students experiencing academic difficulty. Stimuli are reduced, lessons simplified, and creative opportunites cut back. We use more worksheets and repetitive tasks. Instruction is dulled down in an attempt to improve recall. Brain research tells us that we should, instead, fire up the challenges. We retrieve information better when it is connected to our lives. Frank Smith says, "We learn best when we are engaged in an activity that is interesting and meaningful to us, where our past experience is relevant" (1990, 15).

Perhaps if we reconfigure our concept of the brain, we can see why this is so. The brain is more like a gland than a computer. To illustrate, think of the digestive system. Presented with an ice cream sundae or steak, our digestive system goes into immediate action. We are ready to digest the food before it reaches our mouth. Likewise, the brain is constructed to learn and utilize the whole body when encountering a stimulus.

Intelligence is not limited to one narrow band of neurons. Neurobiological research indicates various types of learning activate synaptic connections in different parts of the brain. Howard Gardner (1991) calls these our seven intelligences: language, logical-mathematical, spatial, musical, kinesthetic, interpersonal, and intrapersonal. These intelligences, while different, are used concurrently and complement each other.

Our experience tells us Gardner's view of intelligence makes sense. A girl in our class struggles to write an essay, yet streaks down the basketball court to maneuver for a perfect shot. A boy who has never finished a book in his life rebuilds a motor until it purrs. Brain-based learning recognizes we are born with more than one way to know, and these intelligences enrich each other. Children who study music do better in math. Children who play chess do better in reading.

In addition to plasticity and flexibility, the brain responds emotionally. In our efforts to purify learning, we would like to separate the emotional from the logical, and, incidentally, the creative from the critical. However, brain studies show that the *affective* side of learning is neither a nuisance nor an aberration. Emotion "drives learning and memory" (Sylvester 1995, 72). Those events that we recall most vividly are emotionally laden: a stolen watch, the class reunion. Emotion focuses the mind. When we consider that our survival as individuals and as a species depends on emotion, we can appreciate its importance.

Therefore, when we feel good about ourselves and our surroundings, we learn better. When we set up classrooms to foster success, friendships, and fun, we are doing what the brain craves. Our brains *grow* in a social environment. According to Eric Jensen in *Teaching with the Brain in Mind,* "We are biologically wired for language and communication with one another" (1998, 93).

The new brain theories suggest that our complex of intelligences is developed through social interaction with others, bringing new credence to cooperative learning opportunites as well as problem solving. As a species we are programmed to work together cooperatively, yet schools are generally set up in a competitive atmosphere, ranking children by individual performance and ability (published honor rolls, best grades, best scores).

The brain is designed to work more effectively when information arouses our interest. Under a scanner, segments literally "light up" when a new stimulus enters. Repeated activities, while moving through the brain more efficiently, evince less activity. Does that mean we should drop repetition and memorization? Not at all. Skills improve when they are practiced. However, it does mean that if we limit our instructional methods to those geared for individual progress through a linear progression of skills, we inhibit the natural power of the brain.

How should educators react to these new brain studies? Caine and Caine (1991) in *Teaching and the Human Brain* warn against trying to design lessons that match all of the different styles of intelligence in the classroom. No teacher can adequately deal simultaneously with all of the individual variations. What is needed, instead, is to present students with complex and challenging problems that require critical thinking and social interaction.

Defining Critical Thinking

With our new understandings about the brain, we should not be surprised that the qualities of critical thinking defy neat package labels. Critical thinking does not fit precisely into boxes marked "Logic" or

"Evaluation." Yet both logic and evaluation are aspects of critical thinking. Barry Beyer (1991) takes the philosopher's position when he says critical thinking is discriminating, disciplined, and questioning. The essential components for Beyer are: reasoning, argument recognition, critical judgment, criteria, point of view, dialogue, and dispositions. In *Critical Thinking and Education*, John McPeck defines critical thinking as "the skill to engage in an activity with reflective skepticism" (1981, 152). The NCTE Committee on Critical Thinking and the Language Arts describes critical thinking as "a process which stresses an attitude of suspended judgment, incorporates logical inquiry and problem solving, and leads to an evaluative decision or action" (Tama 1989, 1).

The difficulty with limiting critical thinking to logic, or even suspended judgment, is that these definitions are concerned with justifying a thesis or studying an argument. They do not guide students to discover new problems or to formulate original questions. While reflective skepticism causes us to consider alternatives, make conjectures, and formulate hypotheses, it may not lead us to forge entirely new paths. Frank Smith goes so far as to maintain that "critical thinking is the opposite of logic, it considers all alternatives and resists mechanistic modes of decision-making" (1990, 9). Critical thinking encompasses the "What ifs" of this world through processes that contain elements we currently label "creative."

The relationship between critical thinking and creative thinking is a fascinating one. Creativity has for some time been considered as separate from the intellectual function, and until now IQ test scores have indicated a low correlation between intelligence and creativity. However, current research brings that assumption under question (Chaffee 1994). Creativity is *not* unrelated to intelligence. In fact, solving scientific problems, expressing oneself through art, and thinking critically in general, all depend on rethinking in creative, innovative ways. The psychologist Jerome Bruner (1977) found a complementary relationship between intuitive, or creative, thinking and analytical thinking. Unfortunately, formal school learning has devalued intuition. The best way to encourage effective thinking is to set up an environment where it is all right to take chances, to experiment—and to make mistakes. The following two chapters provide guidelines for establishing such an environment and for involving students in imaginative activities that go beyond logic.

This discussion of the value of intuition and creativity points up another drawback to confining instruction in critical thinking to logical inquiry, evaluation, and a prescribed method for solving problems. For example, while some systematic problem-solving procedures may be better than none, no single method has been found to be consistently superior (Brilhart and Galanes 1989). Strict applications of logical methods, for the most part, are too compartmentalized and ignore the impact of emotions. In the real world, problem solving is far more complicated. People may draw correct conclusions from faulty premises, or reach conclusions intuitively, without any idea how they figured out the answer.

To practice logical thinking methods in isolation has restricted value. In actual living, we always think *about* something. And we need facts upon which to base our conclusions. To that end, we cannot think critically about a subject unless we possess information related to the topic and understand how that influences our interpretation. For example, we cannot evaluate in the same way *Macbeth* and electromagnetism. In studying *Macbeth,* the reader enters the world of the play, discovers its themes, and observes its dramatic structures. Moreover, the reader should also understand character motivation, tragic and comic traditions, and such techniques as dramatic irony. By mulling over these elements, he or she can reach some critical appreciation of Shakespeare's work. However, these evaluative criteria are of little use when applied to electromagnetism. In that case one's hypotheses and conclusions might be based upon both the relationship between electricity and magnetism *and* the way electromagnetism can be applied in an electrical device (say, a motor) to produce motion.

It is interesting to note, on the other hand, the element of commonality in the two processes (that is, understanding *Macbeth* and understanding electromagnetism); both kinds of thinking involve performing abstract thinking, or "operations," to use Piaget's (Piaget and Inhelder 1969, 132) term, upon concrete data. From this perspective, then, we might produce a better definition of critical thinking: *those thought processes that involve more abstract operations.* Applying this definition to classroom activities permits the use of metaphorical comparisons, intuition, the connotation, as well as denotation, of experience. Students are thus freed to symbolize experience in a variety of ways.

Critical Thinking as Abstract Thought

Removing oneself from the here-and-now of experience to express ideas in language is a process of abstraction itself. Interpreting experience, finding commonalities in unrelated happenings, and seeing connections between actual and vicarious events raise concrete realities to the realm of the abstract. The capacity to perceive things in this way can be considered critical thinking because it involves mental decisions and moves the mind beyond mere recall and recognition of facts.

Various levels of abstraction in thinking have been proposed. In his *Taxonomy of Educational Objectives: Book 1 Cognitive Domain,* Benjamin Bloom (1979) identifies comprehension, application, analysis, and synthesis as higher acts of abstraction. Language can have levels of abstraction, as well. In a classificatory scheme, Joan Tough (1979), at the

University of Leeds, described four language functions (the directive, the interpretative, the projective, and the relational) that also foster or promote thinking. These functions are expressed through diverse *uses* of language, such as asking questions, explaining, imagining, predicting, comparing, and reasoning (Tough 1977). In the latter part of this book three thinking skills, reasoning, predicting, and projecting, derived partially from Tough's classification, are explored in detail and form the basis of the structured speech activities presented in Chapter 3.

Abstraction as a Learning Stage

One reason that teachers have difficulty leading students to discover themes in literature is that abstract thinking skills are dependent upon certain developmental factors. Abstract thinking can be thought of as the ability to identify concepts in one set of circumstances and then generalize them to another set of circumstances. According to Jean Piaget (Piaget and Inhelder 1979), children should reach the level of "formal operations" (that is, abstract thinking) at approximately fourteen years of age. The capacity for formal thought evolves over several years. Adolescents just entering the stage would, typically, have more difficulty than older students.

However, maturation may not be the only requisite for abstract thought. Many college instructors find students in their twenties, thirties, or even later, unable to translate concrete facts into abstract generalizations. Chet Meyers (1986), in *Teaching Students to Think Critically*, says the fault lies in our predisposition, at any age, to view the world egocentrically. We all are limited by our own life experiences. Therefore, learning to think critically necessitates moving beyond self, as well as increasing our knowledge about a subject. The ability to entertain alternatives and to suspend judgment is at the core of critical thinking.

On the other hand, children younger than adolescence also display the capacity for abstract thought as evidenced by their natural ability to use metaphors (Gibbs 1995). This research suggests that we are wired to think beyond concrete realities. Whether, as Piaget suggests, individuals move from concrete reasoning to abstract, or whether abstract thinking is always potentially available, we need to expand students' perspectives. Instruction can be structured to make the classroom a catalyst to foster abstract processes. Exercises suggested in Chapter 3, for example, provide students with an opportunity to predict, imagine consequences, and form suppositions. At the same time, by experimenting with different voices, students move from the concrete experience to an abstract level of thought. For this reason, drama activities and discussion are direct contributors to critical thinking.

Drama, Discussion, and Decentering

In the almost-real world of drama, an individual can live safely under several hats and experience others' feelings and viewpoints. The great advantage of drama, or any role-playing activity, is that it moves the student from an egocentric, or self-centered, position to a sociocentered, or other-centered, one. As will become clear, sociocentrism is a necessary condition for abstract thought processes to occur. What might appear to be simply game playing becomes serious business when we recognize that adolescents need this vital step to assist in developing more mature, distanced thinking. When students role-play reporters interviewing Shakespeare about his sources of inspiration, they tap reservoirs of learning. As students simulate congressional debate or dramatize a scene in their own words, they prepare themselves to receive ideas at a more advanced level of thought.

Effective thinkers have the ability to become *decentered* (Britton 1980, 232). They can move beyond themselves and their own limited perceptions. Structured discussion, as well as drama, helps students develop this requirement for abstract thought. Teenagers instinctively like to talk about people, places, ideas, and values. As they attempt to communicate their ideas to others and "try out" new ideas and theories, they leave behind self-centeredness. In discussions, students learn that meanings of words shift with audience. Through trial and error, they discover that ideas they believed were expressed clearly, others interpret quite differently.

This awareness is built through listening skills. Students become conscious of the power of language. Some words have unintended connotations. Their own words trigger surprising reactions. The human mind develops through this process of decentration. By incorporating alternative viewpoints into our own, we develop a model of the world that transcends our own more egocentric viewpoint (Barnes 1976).

James Moffet (1968, 57) links discourse to decentration as a process of movement:

1. from the implicit to the explicit;
2. from addressing the small, known audience to addressing distant and different audiences;
3. from talking about present objects to talking about past or potential objects;
4. from projecting emotion from here and now into there and then;
5. from stereotyping to originality, from groupism to individuality.

Drama and discussion exercises, then, perform dual roles. They allow students to sort through their own understandings of the world while exposing them to the worldviews of their peers. The impact of this social interaction stretches an individual's capacity to absorb new material and sets in motion a dynamic cycle of reviewing and readjusting previously held beliefs.

Speaking, Listening, and Thinking

As a starting point—we must direct our attention to how language, particularly spoken language, affects student thinking. It has been shown that oral language influences the kind of thinking we do (Tough 1980). Using student talk, we can tap students' natural capabilities and channel their innate power to learn, but to some teachers the idea of students speaking freely, even discussing the day's assignment, brings with it the specter of wasted time and undisciplined behavior. However, that need not be the case. If speech activities are carefully structured, if students are aware of the goals, and if the teacher monitors the process as well as the product, talk in the classroom strengthens learning without sacrificing control.

Speech activities such as drama and discussion promote the capability for abstract thinking and, if planned with this end in mind, can become increasingly challenging. Speaking and listening improve not only students' facility with language, but their facility in maneuvering ideas as well. Vague impressions gain reality when they are defined in words. Speech allows ideas to be picked up and examined, set on shelves in categories, and eventually added to other categories, ideas, or words.

Speech has a vital role in children's early development, helping them to construct meanings and to conceptualize the world around them. Naming is crucial during preschool years. Even our concept of self grows through knowing we have a name of our own. Further, naming helps us to categorize the external world. Learning that *kitty* does not stand for all animals is a turning point. Few of us recognize, however, that language continues to define and categorize our world throughout our lives. Language not only increases our lexicon of terminology but also sharpens our perceptions. When we can differentiate a Rembrandt painting from a Matisse, we also absorb concepts about light, color, and design.

Several researchers have addressed the role of speech in cognitive development and have focused on the intrapersonal aspect. Joan Tough's studies, reported in *The Development of Meaning*, initially centered around disadvantaged younger children in England and attempted to discern whether the deprivation of language experiences contributed to subsequent school failure. She found a significant correlation, one that has implications for our own Head Start programs. Tough concluded that the purpose of language in children's development is "that of expressing and constructing meanings, that is, language functions in relation to the child's developing conceptualization of the world about him" (1979, 44).

Words create meanings and build understandings. A deprived language system contributes to a deprived grasp of the world around the child, whether she is three or thirteen. When students are accustomed to the give and take of active discussion, they pay attention to unfamiliar vocabulary. In one class discussion about Doris Lessing's (1976) story "The Witness," a student questions the teacher about a word.

Teacher: Based on what you said earlier, do you think that—Was [Mr. Brooke's] relationship to his dog and his canary the way other people's relationships are to their dogs and canaries? I mean were they intrinsically important to him or not?

Kathy: Explain *intrinsically.*

Teacher: Are the animals important to him because of the companionship they give him, or is it for something else?

Don: I don't think it's for companionship. I think it's because it's for a means of communication.

Kathy: I think he has ulterior motives.

Corrie: Well, I think he just used them to talk about at the office for attention—"My dog did this. My dog did that." And also to bug his landlady. He didn't care about the dog.

Lee: He thought, I guess, it would help with people talking to him.

Kathy: "Oh, what kind of a dog do *you* have?" But, I think he had the pets for ulterior motives. I don't think he really wanted them to love him because he liked pets. I think he wanted them to try and get friends and just to annoy his landlady—for different reasons than maybe were right reasons to have pets.

Language Organizes Experience

Douglas Barnes says, "Teachers have become so habituated to thinking of language in terms of communication that many have ceased to consider that it also performs important subjective functions, since it is the major means by which we consciously organize experience and reflect upon it" (1976, 84). Barnes argues that we grow in understanding by creating representations of our experiences *by* ourselves and *for* ourselves. The speech activities in this book are designed to help students do just that—to enable them to actively make meaning from language rather than passively receive it.

Controlling one's *speech* better enables one to control one's *thought* better. Why this is true is not known at the present. Both speech and thinking are imperfectly understood. Nevertheless, educational researchers support the idea that speech affects thinking skills. L. S. Vygotsky studied young children in an effort to determine the connection. He observed that every psychological development of the child occurred twice: "first on the social level, and later on the individual level" (1978, 57). He also determined that interpsychological behavior (between people) preceded intrapsychological behavior (inside the individual). In other words, first we talk to others, and later we utilize the same speech internally. Without talk, the potential for learning is short-circuited or circumscribed.

This connection between speaking and thinking is easier to understand if we look at a young child. The youngster holds a ball out to his mother and says, "Ball." Later he picks up the ball and says aloud to himself, "Ball." This second use of speech is the intrapersonal one. Later still the boy converts the word to inner speech and what we call "thought." Intrapersonal speech becomes inner speech, or thinking. Once begun, the conversion process continues, aided by frequent input, to develop a unique inner voice.

Interpersonal communication and our experiences are continually transformed into words. We can then use these words as a means to manipulate our thoughts. It is only when we have given form through language to the various influences on our lives that we can make order of our interior worlds. Words, therefore, are the tools of thought. Until we can control the tools, we are unable to control our minds. George Kelly (1963) in his *Theory of Personality* used the term *phrasing* in describing the process of giving form to experience through language. "The problem of learning is not merely determining how *many* or what kind of reinforcements fix a response, or how many nonreinforcements extinguish it, but rather, how does the subject phrase the experience, what recurring themes does he hear, what movements does he define and validations of his predictions does he reap?" (77).

Speaking is intrinsically linked to how we see ourselves. It is not the outside experience that shapes us so much as our ability to shape the experience to fit our own personality. For example, after participating in a drama exercise for *Wuthering Heights,* one of my students observed, "I could feel the rage in Heathcliff. I could feel the disgust he had for Linton and the desire for revenge on Edgar. These things drove him, and I could feel that force when I was saying his words." The drama exercise helped the student to decenter her response to a previously incomprehensible character and to "phrase" the emotions felt by that character.

We mold new experiences to our inner world by language. In discussing an experience, our talk changes the occurrence to fit our present perceptions. We test our understanding of experience with the words we use to explain and describe it. In a discussion of *Wuthering Heights*, students attempt to clarify Heathcliff's behavior:

Laurie: Heathcliff is an example of evil personified. His treatment of Isabella and Cathy proves this.

Kris: No. The cruel way Hindley treated him and Catherine's rejection made him bitter.

John: I think his actions are still too extreme.

As they describe perceptions of the character, these students learn not only to express their views to others, but also to create meaning for themselves.

We do not learn simply by experiencing but by *interpreting* experience. Studying a poem, learning the figures of speech, or reading a novel will remain isolated lessons until the student creates a structure that utilizes the experience meaningfully. As Britton says, "We do not learn from experience left in the raw, unsifted, uninterpreted. Expression, in any form whatsoever, is an interpretation of experience: we learn in the process of expression itself and we learn also from experience made available, brought to hand so to speak, by being expressed" (1982d, 139).

Shaping Thoughts at the Point of Utterance Expressive language, even the mere articulation of thoughts, is necessary for us to classify ideas and theorize about our universe. Contrary to the notion "Think before you speak," we find that it is *when* we speak that creative thoughts are produced. Britton calls this phenomenon "shaping at the point of utterance" (1982c, 139). This spontaneous shaping is an ongoing interpreting process. Speakers usually are not aware as they begin a statement exactly how it will conclude. Speaking aloud releases peripheral information the mind has absorbed and develops the thought more fully.

Rigid rules for expression in the classroom straitjacket thinking, thwart discovery, and prevent intuitive thought. In contrast, sharing ideas freely results in the germination of new concepts. Working together on challenging problems, brainstorming, and participating in open-ended discussions foster the skills of higher abstraction.

Active Learning Versus Passive Learning If indeed we use language to make meaning for ourselves—if understandings are shaped as we speak—then it is apparent that the students are the ones who should be talking in the classrooms not the teachers, who tend to talk for about 70 percent of classroom time. This percentage adds up to something like eight thousand hours of teacher-talk that youngsters listen to during their school years (Cooper 1995). Besides lecturing, teachers ask questions about things they already know and expect short, predictable answers. Students *do* learn under these conditions, but they learn at the lowest common denominator—passive recall. Shifting the focus to student speech does not negate the value of the teacher. It *does*, however, place a responsibility on the teacher to design an environment in which speaking and listening are given equal weight to writing and reading. Educators should realize that competency in these language modes deserves the same disciplined attention currently given to writing and reading.

Without reducing the content of the curriculum or drastically altering materials, we can turn students into active participants. When we change the *process* of learning, a change in emphasis also takes place: the *how* of learning assumes more importance than the *what* of learning. The students become involved in meaning making by verbalizing concepts and by listening more effectively. The teacher promotes critical thinking by listening to students' ideas and by guiding progress.

The following suggestions for incorporating speech into the curriculum help in planning lessons:

1. Use speaking and listening within the content area.
2. State clear objectives.
3. Assign definite time limits and tasks.
4. Give prompt, explicit, and constructive evaluation and feedback.
5. Integrate speaking and listening with writing and reading.

The Social Aspect of Thought

As our view of learning shifts from one that places the primary emphasis on accumulating facts to one of constructing meaning, we realize the importance of social interaction. For a "thinking classroom" the most important element is the social setting. The best way to elicit higher-order cognition is for students to work together in solving problems and designing projects (Resnick and Klopfer 1989). Relationships are the motor that moves academic progress. Students should have time for some social, not just academic, talk, because our minds open when we feel affirmed. The communication climate or the degree to which people see themselves as valued must be supportive because the way students feel about a class profoundly affects their learning. Students work harder and achieve more in classes that are challenging and friendly (Lewis, Schaps, and Watson 1996).

The value of talk in the classroom has been researched under various conditions. A study conducted in a girls' comprehensive school in

South London compared students who used the "talk" method of learning to a group who worked independently on worksheets. The students who discussed the topics showed significantly greater retention than those who worked alone. Between the two groups there was no measurable difference in ability level or the complexity of problems they tackled. The single isolated factor was group discussion (Talk Workshop Group 1982). Cooperative learning while receiving high marks from theorists has not found universal favor, especially by those who believe that gifted children fare better in homogeneous settings. Nevertheless, in a recent study involving 42 teachers and 786 fourth-grade children, it was found that gifted and nongifted children in a cooperative learning environment performed as well on achievement tests as those in homogeneous groups. In addition, academic self-esteem improved for both the gifted and nongifted students (*Cooperative Learning and the Gifted* 1998).

In classrooms where students are encouraged to talk to each other and share ideas, we find a climate of positive energy. The potential for each student increases to the highest level, or the zone of proximal development that Vygotsky (1978) described, where learners' abilities extend to the level of the most advanced. An additional value of group discussion is that strategies learned in groups are transferred to the individual student working alone. The classroom that takes an open approach—hypothesizing, testing, and asking questions—opens up these same techniques to the student when he or she is thinking independently.

The flip side of talking is important, too. Students must learn to listen to each other if they are to learn effectively.

Listening for Comprehension

We listen more than the other three forms of communication. (See Figure 1–1). Yet, we receive virtually no training in listening. An important component for sharing ideas effectively requires that listeners understand messages. However, most people are poor listeners. Research shows that immediately after hearing a message, we remember only about half. That quickly fades, and within time, we remember only a fraction of the original message, or approximately 25 percent. Most of the instructional time is spent on reading and writing, or those activities that occupy proportionately little time compared to listening and speaking. We have allowed listening to become the orphan of education (Wolff et al. 1983).

Although listening has been categorized differently by various scholars, basically, there are four types: informative, critical, empathic,

Figure 1–1
The 1928 Rankin Study (Wolff, F. I., N. C. Marsnik,
W. S. Tacey, R. G. Nichols 1983, 3)

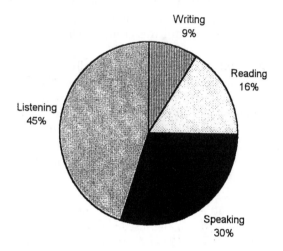

and appreciative. These four types do not operate in isolation. We use elements of informative listening as we listen critically. We often incorporate empathic listening into the other listening types. Just as we think on several levels simultaneously, so do we listen to messages in more than one way. Nevertheless, if we wish to improve listening skills, we can focus on one type of listening at a time and hone its components. In the classroom, the two types of listening we use most often are informative and critical.

Informative Listening My observation of classroom discourse, and of discussion in general, is that informative listening is the most important skill to learn. We leap to judgments all too readily, and none too accurately. Many problems would be avoided, arguments averted, and misunderstandings derailed if we listened to the full message of speakers. People jump to a solution before they understand a problem's full complexity. Our minds race along on our own tracks, thinking of counterarguments, witty comebacks, and a better story. The synapses fairly crackle, but we miss key ideas and overlook the speaker's intent. This ego-centeredness is the great fault of habitual listening patterns.

The goal of informative listening is to receive the thoughts of the speaker with as little distortion as possible. Informative listeners concentrate on main ideas, look for organizational patterns, note key ideas, draw inferences, and delay judgment. Listeners should process information by asking themselves: What did the speaker say? Is it true? If so, then what? Would this be true if? Could I restate it? Do I understand the vocabulary? What is of value to me?

The space between the speaker and listener's rate gives time to record self-questions as mental or written notes. These questions should clarify, not destroy, the speaker's ideas. The goal is not to formulate a rebuttal, but rather to understand fully. As part of our comprehension process, we can suggest examples or rephrase ideas in our own words to test understanding.

Critical Listening Critical listening begins with informative listening, but it goes beyond acquisition of facts to evaluation of the message. As critical listeners, we decide whether to accept, reject, or modify the speaker's ideas. To make these kinds of judgments, we must identify the emotional components, as well as faulty reasoning patterns, problems with evidence, and the speaker's credibility. We need to be familiar with argument structure and to possess background information about the topic. Most important, we must learn to recognize our own worldview bias.

Fortunately, with effort, ineffective listening practices can be overcome. We have to motivate ourselves and our students to value better listening and not leave improvement to chance. In an information society, listening is critical. More than 50 percent of the U.S. national product now comes from people collecting, generating, and using knowledge and information (Speech Communication Association 1989). Industry has become aware of the importance of listening. Executives of major corporations recognize that "poor listening is one of the most significant problems facing business today" (Wolvin and Coakley 1992, 8).

As an aid, this acrostic for the word LISTENS can remind us of the basics for effective listeners.

> Listen without
> Interrupting,
> Stay attentive
> To hidden messages,
> Evaluate after
> Noting all the facts, and
> Send feedback.

The Teacher as Listener

The teacher must not only help students sharpen their listening skills, but also improve his or her own ability. To this end, it is wise to keep the following points in mind. First, it is better to attend to the content of a student's message rather than to the "correctness" of that speech. An emphasis on "proper" language can inhibit the meaning-making process. We should forego insistence on the use of correct technical terms and let discovery of ideas take precedence over precise labeling.

Second, teachers should not worry if students seem to talk over-much, or if they fail to grasp an unfamiliar concept in just one activity. The primary object is to allow students the freedom to express their ideas and examine a problem or concept through different approaches. Rather than our defining results ahead of time, students explore possibilities through trial and error.

In the following transcript, a group of high school students discuss the role of coincidence in the plot of *Tess of the D'Urbervilles*. The teacher might have told them that Thomas Hardy deliberately used coincidence to demonstrate his belief that people are victims of chance. Instead they hunt for meaning on their own:

Matt: Coincidence in this story was just unreasonable. Look at the part—um, when she was on the farms she happens to meet up—let's say the second time she worked on a farm—when was that at—the wheat farm—something like that?

Shawn: It doesn't matter.

Matt: Well, anyway, she's on the farm and here she is and she happens to meet up with two other people she'd been working with on the dairy farm . . . Totally unlikely, totally illogical, and unreasonable . . . And another example of a poor coincidence is where she's walking back from where Mr. Clare lived, and she meets up with Alec, who is now this reformed preacher. What are the chances that of all the places to preach he would choose to preach in some backwoods little place where she never would have stopped in the first place?

Shawn: Well, I have to disagree . . . coincidence is a literary device used by many authors in this period, and you have to realize a couple of facts . . . basically, you are dealing with the 1890s and the mode of transportation was . . .

Matt: Walking.

Shawn: Walking, horse carriages. There were no airplanes, no buses, and you know, one couldn't get around that well. So, you could maybe make twenty miles in one day . . . And Tess's only means of transportation . . . is walking, so she stayed in this twenty-mile radius . . . These are backwoods people. They don't go off jet-setting to London for the weekend . . . So, Jong Soo, what do you think about coincidence?

Jong Soo: There's one aspect, of course, that has nothing to do with transportation . . . It's that as soon as she begins to fall in love with Angel, she's—um—he leaves and she turns to Alec—and when she starts falling in love with Alec then Angel comes back and she changes her mind.

Matt: Exactly—Exactly—They just happen to pop in . . .

These students actively look for incidents to prove their ideas. They test hypotheses and try to find patterns. This small portion of a transcript gives a glimpse of thinking in action. There is another interesting aspect to this discussion. Jong Soo's contributions to the small group are a marked contrast to his usual classroom behavior. Although he was the class valedictorian, he only spoke in class when the teacher called upon him to do so. His responses were brief and barely audible. In the whole class setting, Jong Soo may have been too shy to speak. He also had been taught to be deferential to authority. At Shawn's invitation, he gives a rather lengthy response. Without the presence of an adult, Jong Soo is free to express his ideas. The small group changed the social dynamics.

Besides using structured speech activities related to the course content, students can discuss everyday problems. Allowing teens to talk about issues of concern establishes an open atmosphere and signals the teacher's willingness to be a listener, not just a talker. In that role, he or she can guide students to deal with problems in mature ways. Over the years, my classes discussed the merits of Desert Storm, the loss of parents through divorce, classmates' untimely deaths, hotly contested school elections, new school rules, exam schedules, and, once, a drive-by shooting in the parking lot. At times, administrators were invited into the classes to listen to the youngsters' ideas and to share their own viewpoints. Real tensions were resolved this way. Avenues were found for continued dialogue.

After experiencing a year of discussing issues in small groups and learning to lead whole class discussions, one senior observed that group discussions should begin in ninth grade. "So when you become a senior you don't get all hyped up when someone asks you something."

Another classmate disagreed. She thought ninth grade was too late. Discussion skills should be taught in elementary school. She believed that children who are shy could learn to take part in class discussions. Drawing on her own experience, she had observed teachers select certain kids as leaders in kindergarten, and once that happened, they were the designated leaders throughout their school years. A practice this senior girl perceived as unfair to the rest of them.

Conclusion

The most efficient and effective way for learning to take place is to tap the innate capacities of the learner. Teenagers are naturally curious and creative. Their mode for gaining knowledge is through active participation. When we give students a chance to meld language and life, we help them build bridges to their own worlds. Language and thought are linked, and we need rich language experiences to develop both to their highest capacity. We cannot deal effectively with unfamiliar concepts until we have the words to talk about them. We cannot talk with confidence about new ideas until we have tested them in a variety of ways. Lunchroom and school bus conversation is simply not enough.

All students can benefit from speech activities. Students already speak and listen in our classrooms; we just need to improve the methods. First we should realize the intrapersonal value of speech as a process to improve thinking. Speaking and listening skills not only help us to read, write, and think better, they also have the power to improve academic self-concept. Once we are aware of why speaking and listening raise higher-order cognitition, we can devise ways to promote them. Using open-ended questions and coordinating group projects become more than recipes for classroom dynamics. Teachers who value exploratory speech as well as formal "final-draft" speech learn that their technique is less important than their attitude. Many resources provide hints for improving critical thinking, speaking, and listening. A list is included in Appendix D.

We can create a climate for learning that encourages our students to speak and listen more effectively—and to think critically. Every day youngsters arrive in our classrooms primed with enthusiasm, experience, and emotions. When we utilize those natural ingredients to activate their minds, the distance they may travel is limitless. The boundaries of their universe and of ours expand as we explore together the unknown territory of the human mind.

Two

Communication-Based Learning

The connections between speaking, listening, and thinking are well documented, but teachers need practical ways to bring them together. The three parts in this chapter address key components in building a communication-based learning environment. After a brief description of each element, classroom aids suggest practical applications.

The first section, The Teacher as Communicator, describes the teacher's communication role in the learning process and the need for self-evaluation. The second section, The Classroom Environment, presents ideas for creating a positive climate and developing effective small groups. The third section, Standards for Effective Communication, addresses how standards for communication can be used to foster the kinds of behaviors and attitudes both teachers and students need if we are to foster better thinking.

One purpose of this chapter is to suggest ways standards can link to lessons and how to apply assessments. Assessments should primarily benefit the learners rather than meet some kind of outside accountability. While all three aspects of the communication-based classroom are critical factors if we wish to achieve an active thinking environment, any one topic can be explored individually.

The Teacher as Communicator

The most essential element in any learning situation is the teacher. His or her personality permeates all aspects of classrooms, from bulletin boards and lesson plans to how students interact with each other. When we walk down school corridors, we sense the differences. Some classes are quiet with children sitting in rows, heads bent over books. In others, clusters of students talk about problems and work together on projects. However, we should realize that no one style is *the* correct one. Children can learn in all of these environments.

Although numerous theorists have dealt with teacher effectiveness, the studies have produced mixed results. No one factor has been isolated as the key to more effective teaching. Researchers do agree, however, that classrooms are complex environments. While logic indicates that the most important quality a teacher must possess is knowledge of the subject taught, other equally significant qualities should also be present. Thomas Good and Jere Brophy (1991) categorize these other qualities as *action-system knowledge,* or planning instruction to the greatest advantage—pacing lessons, making decisions, explaining material, and maintaining interest. Most of this action-system knowledge is based on communication, or how well we understand our audience and how we function as communicators. The messages we send both verbally and nonverbally throughout the day affect the youngsters in our classes. Unfortunately, we are largely unaware of ourselves in these communication roles.

Outside observers have noted some consistent patterns in teachers. We dominate classroom communication. Decades of studies confirm this fact. We use approximately 84 percent of communication time (Good and Brophy 1991, 26). We overemphasize factual information and use questions to keep a steady pace rather than trying to elicit higher levels of comprehension. Studies indicate we have more interactions with boys than girls, and that girls ask fewer and fewer questions as they mature (*How Schools Shortchange Girls* 1992). We tend to call on low achievers less often than high achievers.

Since learning is not solely an intellectual exercise and is dependent upon attitudes and feelings, our response to students, our valuing of them, and our interactions with individuals, not just the group, contributes to our effectiveness. To the extent we motivate students to learn, we achieve the most essential learning component.

Students relate good teaching to the teacher's communication style (Cooper 1995). They describe effective teachers as attentive, relaxed, dramatic, friendly, and precise. Ineffective teachers, on the other hand, are perceived as lacking animation, dramatic ability, precision or clarity, and friendliness. In a national study, high school principals also believed communication skills were key factors for effective teaching. They ranked interpersonal communication, as well as other kinds of communication skills, higher than knowledge of curriculum development (Johnson 1994). The ability to involve students in the process of learning requires the skill of listening carefully, adapting to individuals, and presenting messages in a way that interests the audience.

Our style of communication affects the way students feel about us and the courses we teach. It is, thus, inextricably linked to student learning. Another important feature is how our attitude influences our perceptions. If we choose a negative orientation, we tend to describe classroom problems as the students' fault.

1. Students can't do the work.
2. Students don't listen.
3. Students lack motivation to learn.

Conversely, if we choose a positive orientation, we view our problems as challenges to solve. We think of ways we can improve our system of delivery. This orientation leads us to ask questions and to pursue answers. It becomes a way to research in our classrooms. We can ask:

1. How can I structure the class so students will participate more?
2. How can this lesson be designed to encourage students to think and question independently?
3. How can I raise the potential achievement of each student?

With a positive orientation, we view our task in a proactive way, and there are several benefits: (1) Students perceive that we demonstrate empathy toward them; (2) Students view themselves and the school more favorably; (3) Student achievement rises (Cooper 1995, 248).

In a communication-friendly classroom, children are comfortable talking to each other and with the teacher. This kind of atmosphere reduces stress and fosters confidence. It also helps children who are fearful of communication. They receive the necessary assurance to take risks. Discussions are sometimes held in small groups, which is less threatening than speaking before the whole class. Children encourage each other to talk. Mistakes are less personally threatening.

Studies show that shy students do less well academically than their more oral peers. They have lower grade point averages, lower scores on standardized tests, and more negative attitudes toward school. For that reason, we need to be aware of communication barriers, our own and those of our students.

Fear of communication is not limited to children. James Mc-Croskey and Virginia Richmond (1991), of West Virginia University, have made extensive studies about communication anxiety and they report that teachers may be victims of shyness as well. They recommend that teachers take the Shyness Scale (SS) self-test (included in the Practice segment below) to determine their level of anxiety with oral communication. When teachers have discomfort about speaking, they may hesitate to set up an environment that encourages talk. This kind of self-knowledge is an invaluable asset when we attempt to improve communication skills. The activities that follow include suggestions for setting goals, strategies for monitoring communication patterns, and a shyness test.

1. Practice

Checklist of Goals If we wish to incorporate speaking and listening as part of our design for thinking, we must establish a checklist of criteria.

Frequent Speech

1. Every lesson is designed for an oral response.
2. *Every* student speaks *every day.*

Attitudes

1. Both the teacher and students respect oral communication.
2. Students are allowed to reach conclusions and draw inferences that are not predetermined.
3. Exploratory speech (speech that is hesitant or tentative) is valued.
4. Listening is perceived as an important responsibility.

Teacher Skills

1. Use open-ended questions.
2. Prepare effective guidelines for oral activities.
3. Establish clear criteria for evaluation.

Speech Experiences

1. Students have a variety of speaking experiences: formal speech, drama, discussion, and informal conversation.
2. Students experience leadership roles frequently.
3. Students learn to formulate a variety of questions: probing, validating, and open-ended.

Student Skills

1. Students give and receive feedback.
2. Students understand the objectives and tasks of group discussion.
3. Students learn to reason, predict, and project.

2. Target At-Risk Students

Since studies show that low achieving students receive less of our attention than high achievers, we can target at-risk students and change the pattern. To counteract this kind of neglect, for example, identify five "low" students in each class. Then make a conscious effort to give them more opportunities to respond:

- Greet these students each day as they enter the class.
- Consciously increase their wait time.
- Suggest ways to revise incorrect answers.
- Strive to ask inferential rather than "fact" questions.
- Keep a record of progress.

3. Teacher Researcher Questions

We can become researchers in our own classrooms when we set up projects to increase participation. As any researcher, we can use questions to periodically reflect on progress. The following teacher-researcher questions and sample responses demonstrate possible areas to examine.

1. How did the perceived "lows" react when I gave them more frequent response opportunities?

   Response: *They participated more fully, stayed alert, initiated responses more.*

2. What changes did I observe in the perceived "highs" when the "lows" were called on more frequently?

   Response: *I observed no noticeable change.*

3. What example illustrates a behavior change in a targeted student after I implemented more frequent responses?

   Response: *One student who was reticent became more involved and initiated several spontaneous responses.*

4. What positive changes, if any, have occurred in my perceived "lows"? If yes, which of my behavior changes might have brought it about?

   Response: *One targeted low achiever said to me today, "I don't know why, but this is so much easier to read than what we've done before." (We are reading* Macbeth.*) I had noticed the student's improved reading, too. I think that it may be due to the more inferential types of questions I asked.*

5. How did my preparation of higher-level questions affect the quality of my interaction with "low" achievers?

   Response: *I thought of generic type questions relating to literature. I have been working on ways to elicit this kind of higher-level response. For example "If you were the character, what would you do, think, feel?" I notice that students are venturing more imaginative answers, and that more are joining into the discussion.*

4. Shyness Scale (SS)

We need to analyze our own difficulties with communication. Since one in five teachers experiences problems with shyness, or the same proportion as the rest or the population, we can take the Shyness Scale self-test to determine our feelings about communication.

Instructions: Complete the following Shyness Scale. The following four-teen statements refer to talking with other people. If the statement describes you well, circle "YES." If it describes you somewhat, circle "yes." If you are not sure whether it describes you or not, or if you do not understand the statement, circle "?." If the statement is a poor description of you, circle "no." If the statement does not describe you at all, circle "NO." There are no right or wrong answers. Answer quickly; record your first impression.

1. I am a shy person.

   YES   yes   ?   no   NO

2. Other people think I talk a lot.

   YES   yes   ?   no   NO

3. I am a very talkative person.

   YES   yes   ?   no   NO

4. Other people think I am shy.

   YES   yes   ?   no   NO

5. I talk a lot.

   YES   yes   ?   no   NO

6. I tend to be very quiet in class.

   YES   yes   ?   no   NO

7. I don't talk much.

   YES   yes   ?   no   NO

8. I talk more than most people.

   YES   yes   ?   no   NO

9. I am a quiet person.

   YES   yes   ?   no   NO

10. I talk more in a small group (3 to 6 people) than others do.

    YES   yes   ?   no   NO

11. Most people talk more than I do.

    YES   yes   ?   no   NO

12. Other people think I am very quiet.

YES   yes   ?   no   NO

13. I talk more in class than most people do.

YES   yes   ?   no   NO

14. Most people are more shy than I am.

YES   yes   ?   no   NO

Scoring: YES = 1; yes = 2; ? = 3; no = 4; NO = 5.

To obtain your SS score, complete the following steps:

Step 1. Add the scores for items 1, 4, 6, 7, 9, 11, and 12.

Step 2. Add the scores for items 2, 3, 5, 8, 10, 13, and 14.

Step 3. Complete the following formula: Shyness Score = 42 (minus) total from Step 1 (plus) total from Step 2.

Your score should be between 14 and 70.

Scores above 52 indicate a high level of shyness. Scores below 32 indicate a low level of shyness. Scores between 32 and 52 indicate an average level of shyness.

Interpretation: If you scored above 52, it is likely that you are shy and perhaps do not talk a lot. The higher your score, the more shyness you experience, and the less likely you are to be talkative. This suggests that you are quieter than most people. A high score does not necessarily mean that you are afraid to talk, but only that you prefer to be quiet in many circumstances when others would prefer to talk.

If you scored below 32, it is likely that you are not shy and probably talk a lot. The lower your score, the less shy you feel, and the more likely you are to be talkative. A low score means that your own oral activity could dominate the activity of quiet children. You will need to be particularly careful not to be verbally aggressive or to expect your children to become as talkative as you are.

Your score on the SS should give a fairly good indication of your normal oral activity level. If the score does not match your own perceptions of your behavior, talk to someone whom you trust and who knows you well, to see if your friend thinks the scale is accurate.

The SS test can also be used to determine the students' level of shyness. From kindergarten to third grade, the test should be administered orally to individuals. Fourth to sixth graders should also take the test orally, but as a group. After sixth grade, the written test can be given to a whole class. Students gain from this kind of self-knowledge. They learn that everyone experiences shyness under certain circumstances. By talking openly about the problem, we remove the stigma and the mystique of shyness. It is heartening to know that virtually everyone can be helped to become more confident as he or she communicates with others. Learning the skills and practicing them reduces apprehension, and at the same time improves communication competence.

(Shyness Scale from McCroskey & Richmond 1991, 27–30. Reprinted with permission from the National Communication Association.)

The Classroom Environment

Much of classroom activity depends on talk. As mentioned earlier, however, the most frequent form of classroom discussion is teacher-dominated. If we change the emphasis to student-led discourse, we must be aware that good discussions do not happen spontaneously; they are planned. Fortunately, the techniques are not difficult to learn. The first thing to keep in mind is that we must establish a climate of trust, one which gives students the confidence to express their ideas orally. Secondly, no one strategy makes group process effective. Each of us should feel free to experiment with a variety of methods, remembering that what works well for some people may be less successful for others. Third, it is helpful to keep a record of the strategies tried through various means: tapes (both audio and video), journals, observation records, and other methods.

Climate of Trust

We must convey a strongly supportive attitude toward each student. Every person's contributions must be valued carefully, both by the teacher and by that person's classmates. Trust building begins the first day of class and continues throughout the year. The time spent on building attitudes of respect toward the rights of others pays off in all class experiences.

Trust building begins with the belief that students can learn effectively when they are *discovering* facts rather than just being *told* them. We must allow the unexpected to occur and learn to be comfortable planning for the *how* as well as the *what* of lessons. The following guidelines help create a stable climate of trust:

1. Share responsibility with the students for learning.
2. Allow students to take significant responsibility for their own learning.
3. Facilitate learning instead of directing it.

4. Shape the learning situation instead of dominating it.

5. Demonstrate a positive attitude toward speaking and listening.

6. Model language use: read literature aloud, deliver short impromptu speeches, and tell stories.

7. Welcome students' questions.

8. Provide a variety of oral language experiences.

Building Effective Groups

The regular classroom can accommodate a number of simultaneous speaking activities. Students who jog, do homework, and eat meals while attached to stereo headphones can learn to work in a classroom where four or five groups are talking at once. In each group, theoretically, only one person should be talking at any time. Having students discuss in pairs instead of groups of four may be a good way to begin. Pairing usually makes for a quieter discussion and allows more time for individual participation.

When rapport is established between the members of a pair, you can combine pairs to form groups of four. It is better to vary the composition of the groups, at least at first. By working with different people on different tasks, students eventually find their own learning styles. Sloppy or careless attitudes can develop when the same three or four people work together for prolonged periods.

One of the most important criteria is to give the groups real tasks to perform, real problems to solve. Setting time limits also helps keep groups on task, reduces noise level, and promotes productive conversation. Time creates a framework and aids concentration. It is desirable to give warnings a minute or two before the time elapses to help students plan more effectively.

The group process contains many opportunities for increasing speaking skills, listening competency, and critical thinking. We can understand better how to foster these skills if we divide the parts of small group process into the three P's: *Preparation, Practice, and Playback.*

Preparation

1. The teacher assigns students some type of pre-discussion responsibility. These may be journal notes, free writings, graphics, selected readings, written responses to readings, or research for the group discussion.

2. Students join groups according to the purpose of the lesson.

3. Groups explore the demands of the task and establish criteria.

4. One member of each group reports out to whole class.

5. The teacher posts these requirements as a guide. Each group may have a separate list, or they can compile a single list for the whole class.

Practice

1. Individuals present their ideas in an equitable manner.

2. Group members listen to the speaker's complete message without interrupting.

3. When the speaker has finished, group members respond in turn with constructive comments, questions, or requests for more information. In this way, students practice the skills of listening, sharing, and valuing others' comments.

4. A recorder keeps notes about the shared information.

5. The group prioritizes information.

Playback

1. Groups report to the class through informal or formal presentations.

2. Listeners determine the information's accuracy and completeness through questions and checks for understanding.

3. Listeners compare information to the task demands and criteria.

4. Listeners and speakers refine or expand ideas.

5. Listeners take notes, write in journals, or produce free responses.

6. Speakers and listeners evaluate both the process and products.

7. The whole class or individual groups determine the next step.

Group leadership should rotate. Expectations change when leadership changes. One person may insist on details, another may be more creative. Students interact differently as well. A student who is a non-leader in whole-class activities may function well in directing a small group.

Make sure students know their responsibilities as members of a group. These roles are explained in more detail below. I have found an easy way to help establish turn taking is by assigning each person a letter alphabetically and then ask that they speak in a clockwise manner. That is, A speaks first. The other members of the group are informative listeners. They give feedback and may ask clarifying questions. Next B speaks, and the others follow the same procedure. C speaks, and then D. (See Figure 2–1.)

Looking over notes I've made while teaching students to work in groups, I find comments such as "The smaller the group, the better" and "Rapport is good, not only between the students and me, but also among themselves." The key to effective group discussion is to reduce

Figure 2–1

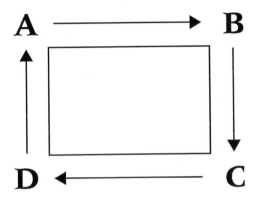

the feeling of risk and to increase feelings of well-being. If the activity is successful, self-esteem rises and students learn the benefits of supporting each other.

Requiring students to produce something (a written observation, a report, or a project) also helps to foster meaningful talk. If space is limited, one group can work in the hall outside the classroom. If you have access to another room, a group can work there. Audiotaping group discussions is useful to monitor their effectiveness, whether in the classroom or outside. Usually, however, it is better to keep all groups working in the same room. This allows you to easily visit and keep track of all of the group processes.

Practice

A Method of Teaching Group Process Secondary students are generally turned off by group-process practice sessions in which specific roles are assigned (for example, gatekeeper, facilitator, and summarizer). They regard these exercises as "time-off" games. Using actual content material imbues the discussion with a real purpose and motivates genuine response.

One way to get students "turned on" to group discussion is by involving them in current issues that relate to literature. In conjunction with *To Kill a Mockingbird*, for example, ask the class to write a ten-minute free response to an open-ended question: "How do racial relations today compare to the 1930s?" or "How much of a problem is racism now?"

Before breaking into groups for discussion, hand out a list of tasks for leaders and members of a group. Briefly discuss how each type of behavior fosters successful group process. I do not include the negative behaviors since they virtually disappear when the positive ones are emphasized. Furthermore, a lot of "acting out" is a symptom of shyness. Thus, efforts to diminish anxiety help students manage their fears and their behavior better.

Group Discussion Tasks

I. Leadership Tasks (Although these are the special jobs of the discussion leader, everyone should practice them.)
  - Initiate discussion.
  - Allow members the equal right to speak.
  - Keep the group on topic.
  - Focus on issues.
  - Probe for answers.
  - Summarize the conclusions of the group.
  - Maintain control.

II. Group Tasks—Each member should:
  - Play a positive role.
  - Provide information.
  - Ask questions.
  - Keep on task.
  - Analyze—Listen for details.
  - Synthesize—Listen for the big picture.
  - Listen actively.
  - Cooperate with other members to reach the common goal.

Form small groups, preferably of four or five students each. Give students a Group Discussion Listener Response form (Figure 2–2) on which they can record the date, the subject under discussion, and their comments. Appoint student A in each group to be leader and allow the groups to discuss their ideas. Using the format previously explained, students A, B, C, and D should read their free responses to the film, each in turn. As listeners, they record notes about the content of the discussion: key ideas, facts, and questions. They should also respond to the speakers. After ten minutes, stop the discussion.

At this point, have the students evaluate their own performances and their observations of others on the Group Discussion Tasks check sheets (Figure 2–2). Under Comments, they should record specific behaviors and statements of group members. Next the group should share with each other what they observed about the discussion. Circulate around the classroom to help groups over rough spots. After the groups have exchanged observations, the whole class can formulate a list of suggestions for effective discussion.

Figure 2–2
Sample Evaluation Forms

Group Discussion Listener Response

Name: Date:

Topic: (How much of a problem is racism now?)

Key Ideas:

Facts:

Questions:

Group Discussion Tasks

Circle the Tasks You Performed		*Circle the Tasks You Observed Others Perform*	
Initiate Discussion	Play Positive Role	Initiate Discussion	Play Positive Role
Help Equalize Turns	Provide Information	Help Equalize Turns	Provide Information
Keep Group on Topic	Ask Questions	Keep Group on Topic	Ask Questions
Focus on Issue	Keep on Task	Focus on Issue	Keep on Task
Probe for Answers	Listen for Details	Probe for Answers	Listen for Details
Summarize Ideas	Listen for Big Picture	Summarize Ideas	Listen for Big Picture
Maintain Control	Cooperate to Reach Goal	Maintain Control	Cooperate to Reach Goal

Comments:

The fact that they "own" the guidelines makes students more aware of expectations. Almost without exception, classes decide they favor leaderless groups with everyone assuming the leadership tasks. If a leader is needed, the position may be shared or rotated. In just one period, you can teach the positive aspects of group dynamics without moralizing. Once everyone is comfortable with small groups, you can use them to activate a persuasive essay, set up a project, analyze a literary work, or initiate a unit.

Standards for Effective Communication

Our goal in teaching English is to enable students to communicate fluently and effectively in all of the language modes, speaking, listening, writing, and reading. While we do not teach skills in isolation, one may be emphasized more than another in a given lesson, or portion of a lesson. To help our focus on the skills of speaking and listening, we need to determine standards for achievement.

American English teachers over the past decades have developed and implemented standards for writing. These standards emphasize areas of concern: originality of thought, vocabulary, structure of messages, and mechanics, to name a few. Based on these components, we have constructed rubrics for measuring achievement. In some instances, we have produced scales so reliable whole departments have used them, even for portfolios or other complex bodies of work. This effort has gone on for decades, involving thousands of hours. It is no wonder that English teachers have not placed the same kind of concentration on evaluating speaking, whether discussion or platform performance.

U.K. Speaking/Listening Standards

In Chapter 1, we discussed how educational organizations, political institutions, the public, and school districts believe that speaking and listening should be included in language arts instruction. Thus, although all forms of English should be taught in an integrated manner, attention must be specifically directed to the quality of speaking/listening literacy.

If we need to find a precedent, we can look across the Atlantic to the United Kingdom (U.K.) where the National Curriculum specifically includes listening and speaking with set requirements for achievement. Teachers are responsible for assessing student progress in the National Curriculum according to Key Stages and Levels of Attainment (Key Stage 3 and 4 is included in Appendix C). At the end of each Key Stage, students sit for national exams. It is expected that students in grade 9 pass Key Stage 3 with an achievement range between Level 3 to 7. Students in grade 11 are expected to pass Key Stage 4. In addition, teams inspect schools to determine how well they are implementing the National Curriculum and to offer recommendations for improvement.

The Office for Standards in Education (OFSTED) gives reports to the individual schools and releases general information to the public about its findings. Of particular interest are the observations related to speaking and listening (*Subjects and Standards* 1996).

- Students achieve the best standards when they speak about worthwhile topics.
- Better discussions usually result when the talk focuses on issues arising from students' reading.
- Many twelve- and thirteen-year-old students are unable to listen with sufficient degree of concentration and discrimination in Key Stage 3.
- Students in Key Stage 3 make little progress in drama, while those in Key Stage 4 achieve high standards. [Drama performance is a part of the curriculum.]
- There is a substantial weakness in recording students' progress in reading, speaking, and listening.
- Bilingual students' performance remains restricted by underachievement in literacy.
- Few schools are well advanced in the use of information technology (IT).

As a result of the 1994–95 inspections, OFSTED makes the following recommendations that have implications for U.S. schools.

- Schools need to train students in the skills of listening.
- Students should be taught to adopt appropriate styles and language when speaking for different circumstances.
- Students, especially in Key Stage 3, must learn to improve their powers of concentration (thinking skills).
- Teachers should find ways to keep effective and usable records of progress in speaking and listening.

Practice

A recent two-year study of outstanding U.S. high schools reports that experts agree that "emphasizing high standards is the cornerstone of educational excellence" (Vladero 1999, 52). Similar findings were reported in the United Kingdom ("School Evaluation Matters" 1998, 1).

Therefore, it is essential to set and maintain standards for performance, whether self-made or from an outside source. They serve as a road map for planning where and how far we want students to go. The following list of standards for speaking and listening are derived from those developed by the National Council of Teachers of English (NCTE) and International Reading Association (IRA), National Communication Association (NCA), and United Kingdom (U.K.).

Standards for Speaking and Listening in English Language Arts

1. Students demonstrate the ability to talk for different purposes to different audiences, using appropriate levels of content, language, delivery skills, and sensitivity to cultural diversity.

2. Students participate effectively in discussions.

3. Students understand and critically respond to print, nonprint, media, and information technology (IT) sources.

4. Students effectively use speaking and listening skills to create meaning, develop ideas, and make decisions.

5. Students demonstrate communication competence in the development and maintenance of personal relationships.

6. Students demonstrate the ability to control communication anxiety.

7. Students demonstrate the ability to listen effectively for a variety of purposes.

8. Students identify problems, conduct research from a variety of sources, and organize findings into an effective message that informs or persuades an audience.

9. Students demonstrate an understanding of active listening by questioning, summarizing, and paraphrasing spoken messages.

10. Students use a variety of media and IT resources to gather and synthesize information and to create and communicate knowledge.

Levels of Achievement Once we have determined standards, then we must consider the various levels of performance that lead to competent literacy. Each standard needs Levels of Achievement to define a progression of skills and place an abstract concept into more concrete terms. These Levels of Achievement provide descriptions of a range of behaviors, enabling students to more clearly understand the objectives. Each level calls for more sophisticated skills. However, it is possible to have great flexibility in determining exactly which level should be designated as a "passing" score.

The goal could be for a certain percentage of students to reach the highest level, and some students, undoubtedly, would exceed that level, especially those who have had experience in leadership roles, drama, or competitive speaking. To challenge those students, a Level X could be added which includes participation in public forums and requires more advanced use of language.

To see how we might design Levels of Achievement, we will use Standard 2 above: "Students participate effectively in discussions." Obviously, many components are required for effective participation in a group. Without training, group discussions can take on the worst features of a Jerry Springer TV talk show. On the other hand, with guidance and practice, even quite young children can engage in productive group discussions. The following Levels of Achievement reflect the idea that effective discussion necessitates that people must be willing to entertain more than one point of view, and they must intend to expand their understanding of the topic. James Dillon (1995) addresses the requirements for true discussion in *Using Discussion in Classrooms.* He recognizes that discussion is a progression of skills.

> From a developmental point of view, a class might meet these conditions [for true discussion] to progressively greater extent. For instance, more students talk in the discussion and students talk more; students listen more carefully and over more extended time; their contributions are more responsive to what others are saying, and more frequently related to the preceding contribution; they are more purposeful in talking for understanding the topic under discussion. (9)

An Example of Levels of Achievement for Speaking and Listening: The following levels of achievement for the above Standard 2, "*Students participate effectively in discussions,*" reflect a progressive development in the skills of discussion. For this type of growth to occur, more instructional strategies are required than to merely introduce a list of skills. The classroom must establish and maintain a climate of trust that encourages students to participate.

Level 1: Students talk and listen in discussions to explore and communicate ideas. They show awareness of the tasks needed to make group interaction effective. They ask relevant questions, focus on the topic, and contribute ideas. They practice turn taking and do not interrupt the speaker.

Level 2: Students talk and listen in an increasing range of contexts. They show competence in helping the group develop ideas by asking questions, keeping on task, and providing information or opinions. As active listeners, they support speakers with feedback, stay attentive for details, and look for the big picture. They demonstrate an attitude of cooperation for the group task. They respect other people and their ideas.

Level 3: Students talk and listen in a wide range of contexts. They understand the need for clarity and precision in the expression of meaning. They use the skills of informative listening to determine main ideas. To ensure the validity of messages, they evaluate the use of sources, reasons, and evidence. They understand and use the structure of argument. They rephrase ideas for better understanding, summarize material for clarity, and display open-mindedness to the opinions of others.

Level 4: Students take an active part in the leadership of the group. They encourage participation by group members, initiate discussion, equalize opportunity, and help promote the process of discussion. They make significant contributions to the content and the process. As listeners they display empathic listening skills as well as those necessary for informative and critical listening.

Level 5: Students are confident participants in discussion, regardless of whether their role is one of leader or participant. They assist the group to explore a topic in depth. They can present persuasive arguments as conclusions with supporting data. They can evaluate complex ideas, solve problems, and adapt ideas to accommodate new information. They are competent in all of the leadership and group process tasks. As listeners, they demonstrate the ability to select the most effective type of listening for the situation.

Assessment

A serious problem with determining the levels of achievement levels is that assessment of oral communication, by its very nature, inhibits the qualities we wish to promote—an openness of interaction, reduced speech anxiety, more confidence and fluency. For that reason, assessment should take the form of feedback during the speaking and listening processes, as much as possible. We can use student self-evaluations and reflections, peer responses, and various describing methods as part of the evaluation.

Another problem is that speaking activities present a difficult challenge. Speech is more transitory than writing, and to be effective, most of the evaluation and feedback have to be done in the middle of the action. To do these tasks well requires practice as well as patience.

We face other dilemmas. In a discussion before the whole class, John is quiet and appears to contribute little. Is this because he is daydreaming, unprepared, or shy? If it is the last reason, and he is one of those children for whom shyness is a real problem, should he be marked low? And what of Melanie? She delivers long, well-documented messages with clear articulation. Should she receive a high score when she appears to eclipse others' ideas? And what of Andrew? He has researched his topic more thoroughly than anyone else and his group members benefited from his research. Yet in the discussion, he ignores turn taking. On the other hand, while Jennifer's contributions are as light as a birthday balloon, she inspires her group to do their best. These are all problems I have encountered. In the interest of fairness, I now avoid a single score.

It is more desirable to provide a number of opportunities for speaking and listening, and use the accumulated evidence in the evaluation process. Besides a writing folder, students can keep a speaking/listening folder with samples of listening notes, checklists for group discussion, journal entries, self-goals, and reflections on progress. During discussion, quiet students can write questions and comments they do not have a chance to ask. Students can keep records of speech preparation. They can make tapes of talks and discussions. Keeping records of experiences like these, we can accumulate documentation of progress toward the standards.

Since assessment should be as open as the kind of thinking we wish to promote, students should be aware of, and if possible co-participants in designing, the methods. At the beginning of any assignment, the specific criteria should be spelled out in detail. If listening feedback or peer critiques are part of the evaluation, that requirement must be stated clearly. Fairness demands that all of the goals we set for students and our means for determining whether or how well they are reached should be set squarely before them. Rubrics should be explained and exemplars examined. Classroom assessments must be perceived as fair or that hard-won climate of trust evaporates.

Assessment Suggestions Many of the activities in Chapter 3, "Critical Thinking Skills and Activities," can be thought of as steps in a process, ways to generate ideas, or means to review subject matter. Your evaluation of products—whether it is a paper, a test, or a project—should include recognition of these interim activities. Although the goal is to foster one or more of the standards and to indicate progress in the Levels of Achievement, it is not always necessary to assign a number or letter grade. Narrative evaluations are effective replacements for objective scores much of the time. Written comments increase students' self-confidence even while their performances are being compared to the desired levels of achievement.

Your role as an active listener allows you to be totally involved. The projected goal of having 100 percent student participation in oral communication will be reached only if students feel your support and respect. Thus as an observer, you can recognize the silent student for his or her journal reflections, notes, eye contact, and friendly reaction to other members. Our positive comments create better growth than negative criticism:

"You asked two questions today."

"Your summary statement advanced discussion."

"Your comparison of realism in *The Color Purple* to *To Kill a Mockingbird* changed the focus of the discussion."

This sort of support and feedback enhances awareness of the process and increases students' perception of the goals and value of speaking and listening. Together, you take responsibility for becoming collaborators in making meaning.

Questions to Ask About the Assessment Process Think about your particular course, class, or program in regard to the assessment process. Answer the following questions as you develop an assessment program:

1. What are your purposes for engaging in assessment and generating assessment data? (to advise students, to redirect content and pedagogy, to address accountability)

2. What type of data would best accomplish those purposes? (quantitative, qualitative, descriptive, student-generated)

3. What aspect of learners' behaviors do you want to assess? (cognition/information, behaviors/performance, affect/feelings)

4. How will you assess/evaluate those behaviors? (existing instruments, develop your own tools, alternate forms)

5. What alternative forms of assessment have you used/considered? (peer assessment, self-assessment, journals, oral performance, portfolios, videos, audiotapes, projects)

Conclusion

It may be apparent by now that communication-based learning involves who we are, how we perceive and interact with students, and how we design and measure standards of performance. The focus shifts to the role communication plays in much of what we now take for granted. Students need to see themselves and their ideas as respected and valued. They need to care about themselves and each other. Everyone benefits from such a climate, and we become free to take the risk of more adventurous thinking.

The dynamics of learning become exciting for both teacher and students because all of the answers are not predetermined. There are expectations, however, that include honesty, sincere effort, and respect for every person. If we want youngsters to risk failure in their endeavors, we must be willing to risk not knowing all of the answers ourselves. When we join students in discovery, we become facilitators and guides, a position that may make us uncomfortable at first.

This approach requires time and is more demanding than plotting a traditional lesson. The benefits are that in the end, we can see that altering our method pays off in several ways. First, we are often richly rewarded with our students' progress. Second, our own learning expands in unexpected directions. Third, we are no longer limited by past practice and can explore new routes into familiar subjects. With the new learnings, we, as well as our students, become different people.

Three

—

Critical Thinking
Skills and Activities

Critical thinking as it is used in this book applies to those processes requiring more abstract thought. When we use language to build ideas, discover reasons, explore possible consequences, and imagine events, we engage in critical thinking. Sharing language experiences, we create schema, develop new patterns, and remodel old ones. The brain works on many levels at the same time. The logical side of our mind is present all the while, determining which ideas fit, which should be discarded. This section explores three types of critical thinking: reasoning, predicting, and projecting. For each, activities in listening and speaking are recommended to reinforce the skills.

Reasoning

All critical thinking is not based on argument; nevertheless, by learning the principles of sound reasoning, we give students tools they can use in the real world. Fitting ideas together, seeing one event as the cause of another, perceiving a concept as being more significant than another, and recognizing similarities and differences are all applications of the thinking skill we call "reasoning." Reasoning is no easy matter. At first glance, cause and effect may seem to be quite straightforward. In reality situations are usually affected by many factors. A tree falls in our backyard during a violent storm, and we assume wind was the major cause. Instead, the tree's root system may have been weakened by injury or decay, and its "time had come." We must take into account not only the readily observable but also coincidence and alternate causes.

Because of these variables, cause and effect has been called "the most complex form of reasoning." (Fryar, Thomas, and Goodnight 1989, 61). While this assessment of cause and effect is accurate, its use is pervasive and can create a great deal of mischief. Simply because a statement "sounds" right, people believe, and we frequently hear, comments such as:

Laziness causes people to live on welfare.
The teachers' powerful unions cause school failure.

Sound reasoning can be taught in the classroom as an antidote to accepting such statements at face value. We will explore two techniques that develop skill in reasoning. These are question making and debate.

Question Making

Question making must be taught. Although we acknowledge that question asking is essential for learning, as educators we are the ones who traditionally dominate questioning in the classroom. We have a strong distrust of relying on student questions to develop a lesson. We wonder:

- How can students question if they lack knowledge?
- Won't their questions be trivial?
- Won't their questions be of a lower level that those of the teacher?

My studies indicate that the vast majority of student questions are serious and worthwhile (O'Keefe 1988). When we place responsibility on our students, they respond to that trust and perform at higher levels than we might suppose. My experience is not unique. Robert Marzano (1992) makes the same observation in A Different Kind of Classroom: Teaching with Dimensions of Learning.

Students should learn the difference between closed and open-ended questions. By their very nature, open-ended questions lead to higher-level abstract thinking. Such questions can be used to explore almost any topic in any school subject, and students can learn to construct different formats. Consider these generative questions:

1. How would you feel . . . [about the attack on Pearl Harbor], if you were . . . [living in Hawaii at the time]?
2. What if . . . [you were the survivor of a nuclear holocaust]?
3. How would you react if . . . [you arrived in America as an immigrant in 1896]?
4. As the author of . . . [1984], how did you decide on the setting?

Questions of this type force both the questioner and the answerer to treat the subject matter in new ways. If the questioning is really imaginative, everyone becomes caught up in the work of translating unfamiliar material into terms that are easier to understand. Once students learn these techniques, they have less trouble "digesting" new ideas, and it is easier for the teacher to spot areas that block students' comprehension (misunderstandings about time periods, lack of background information, and fuzzy or faulty notions). Using open-ended questioning, students will actually cover a topic in more depth than when following the "stick-to-the-lesson" textbook approach.

To ensure that the necessary content is covered, assign groups, rows, or pairs of students to prepare questions on particular areas of the subject, such as: characterization, setting, theme, plot, and symbolism. You can then begin the discussion by modeling a few open-ended questions. Once students grasp the idea, they may devise quite provocative questions. For example, students generated the following questions about *Emma* by Jane Austen:

Characterization: How does Emma's manipulation of Harriet compare to Mrs. Elton's manipulation of Jane?

Setting: If you were to produce *Emma* as a modern-day American film, where would it take place and why?

Theme: What is Austen saying about the role of women, and does it have relevance today?

Plot: How can you compare *Emma* to a modern-day soap opera?

Symbolism: Select an image from the first chapter of *Emma*. Why is that image significant throughout the novel?

As students manufacture questions, they use their own previous knowledge of the subject. They simultaneously review information and apply it to the new situation. They also test their own perceptions against those of their classmates.

Another method of constructing open-ended questions is to take textbook questions and ask students to twist them around into new formats. This allows students to "play" with questions, as in the following instance:

Textbook question: Why did Shakespeare not have Lady Macbeth appear in Act IV?

Reformatted question: Imagine that Lady Macbeth appeared in Act IV in a prominent role. How would she have behaved?

Among the responses were:

"Perhaps Lady Macbeth would call a messenger to send a message to Lady Macduff, but he would refuse. This would show her loss of power."

"I think that including Lady Macbeth in Act IV might have heightened the tragedy of the slaughter of Lady Macduff and her children."

Debate and Argumentation

Debate and formal argumentation are an extension of questioning tactics in the reasoning process. These traditionally competitive activities can be adapted to noncompetitive, nonspecialized instructional situations. When groups of students prepare arguments, there is less personal risk. Discussion is more active and effective, with the added plus that everyone has more fun.

The problem-solving process usually follows a sequence similar to that outlined by John Dewey (1910). It is necessary first, to explore the background of the problem; second, to identify the causes of the problem; third, to isolate the possible solutions and determine the best one; and fourth, to plan a way to implement the solution. Each of these steps requires using higher levels of abstraction.

We do not have to look far to find topics for debate. In today's classroom it is desirable, if not essential, to deal with the social, political, and economic problems of this and other days. Much of our literature relates to these issues and provides a fruitful opportunity for study. Teen pregnancy, alcoholism, poverty, racism, child abuse, and gender issues are just a few. However, students need guidance as they attempt to analyze problems. First of all, they must break a whole into several parts. To analyze the causes of the problems mentioned above, they would have to examine economic, political, social, historical, and psychological issues. Students must learn how to question apparently true positions, proposals, and facts. Too often, public opinions are derived less from fact and more from media hype or national prejudice. To achieve a more thorough examination of a problem, students need to pursue the following types of questions:

1. What is the extent of the problem?
2. What factors caused the problem?
3. What solutions can correct the problem?
4. What solution would be the best and for what reason?
5. What solution is the most consistent with American traditional values?

Argumentation Theory

Arguments are not won because one person shouts louder than the other, despite being given that impression by many TV talk shows. The basic criterion for assessing the relative value of one argument over another is that the better argument is supported by better facts, examples, and proofs. In addition to data, the argument must be organized logically, that is, the evidence relates directly to the claim being made. For example, it is not enough to assert that the lack of bilingual education causes many Latino students to drop out of school; it must also be shown that no other factor causes the high dropout rate. Relationships must be drawn through comparison, cause and effect, and accurate statistical analysis. Students must learn to pay attention to the source of statements used as evidence, the time at which the data was collected, and whether the information fits the present circumstances or state of knowledge. For instance, a physician (good source) states in a 1980 magazine article (probably outdated data) that stress is the cause of stomach ulcers. Subsequent medical research has found a bacterial source (current information overrides old data).

Students must keep the following criteria in mind when preparing for debate: (1) assertions must be supported with valid evidence, (2) information must be accurate and documented (title, author, and date), and (3) chains of cause and effect must be logical. While the demands of speaking and writing differ, practice in researching topics and organizing information in this kind of logical order speeds students' writing of persuasive essays and improves written research papers as well.

Debating Propositions of Policy or Fact

Propositions of fact may be debated. At first glance, this is the easiest kind of debate. Fryar, Thomas, and Goodnight say the purpose of this type of debate is "to determine (1) what occurred, (2) what data are required to establish the alleged fact, and (3) what data is available for use" (1989, 20–21). Examples of debatable propositions of fact are:

Macbeth is insane.

King Arthur was a historical figure.

The earth is warming.

Propositions of policy can be more complex. Just what constitutes a policy? A policy in debate relates to the design and implementation of actions, rules, regulations, or laws determined by governmental bodies. Issues that involve spending, law and order, domestic concerns, and commerce fall within the boundaries of policy, whether national or local. Policies may be totally new or they may be old ones altered to fit new conditions. The advantages and disadvantages of such policies are the concern of debate. Examples of debatable propositions of policy are:

Bicycle riders must wear helmets.

Taxes on food should be eliminated.

A "Family Living" course should be required for high school graduation.

In order to defend positions on a proposition, students must learn about both sides. The person holding the negative position does more than refute the affirmative position; he or she also presents a constructive argument on the opposite side of the resolution. The structure of the argument is: a thesis statement, definitions, three or four supporting facts with examples, and a conclusion. (See Figure 3–1.)

Besides the fuller understanding that such exploration entails, the value of classroom debate is that students learn to *listen* to arguments, compare proposals, differentiate between opinion and fact, and discern sound argument from rhetoric.

Debating Propositions of Value

Lincoln-Douglas debate, one of the reasoning activities that follow, is based on the famed confrontations between Abraham Lincoln and Stephen Douglas. The difference between Lincoln-Douglas debate and traditional debate is that Lincoln-Douglas debate involves propositions of value rather than policy. Propositions of value are based on opinions and attitudes. While they are judgments about the qualities of a person, place, thing, idea, or event, they are grounded in truths derived from philosophy, psychology, sociology, and moral traditions.

When reading *The Heart of the Matter* by Graham Greene, students could debate a Lincoln-Douglas topic, such as "Resolved: When in conflict, individuals should value their own conscience over the law."

In arguing this type of resolution, less emphasis is placed on statistically based evidence and more on various hierarchies of value: social, political, or humanistic. Lincoln-Douglas debate is admirably suited for a classroom as a way to study in depth the issues that confront characters and influence their situations.

Reasoning Exercises

While several of the standards mentioned in Chapter 2 apply to the following six activities, we will use Standard 8 (40) as a model: "*Students identify problems, conduct research from a variety of sources, and organize findings into an effective message that informs or persuades an audience.*"

These exercises are designed to develop skill in the following broad areas: perceiving relationships, cause and effect, problem solving, comparison and contrast, and classification of schemata.

Figure 3–1
Sample Outline

Planning the Speech

Organize your thoughts into an outline.

Topic: _____

Title: _____

Thesis Statement: _____

I. Introduction:

    A. (Attention-getter)_____

    B. (Definitions)_____

    C. (Thesis)_____

II. Body:

    A. (Fact One)_____

        1. (Example)_____

        2. (Statistics)_____

    B. (Fact Two)_____

        1. (Example)_____

        2. (Statistics)_____

    C. (Fact Three)_____

        1. (Example)_____

        2. (Statistics)_____

III. Conclusion:

    A. (Summary)_____

    B. (Call to Action)_____

Reasoning Exercise 1: Round-Robin Questions

Objective: To develop students' ability to generate questions concerning relationships, cause and effect, and reordering of information.

Approach: This activity assists students in performing inductive analysis on a novel, chapter, or unit of work. Assign groups of students to work independently on devising open-ended questions. If the subject is a novel, one-fourth of the class might think of questions relating to plot conflict; one-fourth, characters; one-fourth, setting; and one-fourth, symbols or imagery. The questions can invite personal responses: "Which scene was most vivid and why?" "If you were going to write a letter to the main character about his decision, what would you tell him and why?" "What mistake did the author make?"

After allowing students five minutes to generate questions, have them write responses to their own questions (another five minutes). Then divide the class in half and place the students in two semicircles facing each other. Person 1 on Team A asks person 1 on Team B his or her best question. Person B-1 answers, then A-1 evaluates the answer and says what his or her answer would have been. Next, A-2 asks B-2 a question, and the process continues until all of Team A's questions are completed. Students on Team B then ask Team A their questions.

Advantages: The questions and this method encourage divergent thinking, active participation, and many tests of relationships.

Variations:

1. Alternate sides in asking questions.
2. Anyone on Team B can answer A's questions, otherwise the process stays the same. When Team B asks questions, anyone on Team A may answer.

Assessment: Assign one member of each team to summarize the information received in response to their questions. Students listen to the summaries and add or edit information. Students determine as Teams or the whole class what, if any, additional information is needed.

Reasoning Exercise 2: Concoct-a-Question

Objective: To generate as many questions as possible in a fixed amount of time and to increase students' perception of relationships within a body of material.

Approach: Divide the class into groups of five. Tell the class that each group is responsible for concocting an unlimited number of questions in ten minutes about a selected topic. In this brainstorming session, no question will be too ridiculous or too simple. After ten minutes, have the groups select the ten best questions generated.

Next, direct the groups to form a large circle. Have all the A's sit together, all the B's, and so on. A-1 asks B-1 the first question from Group A's list. If B-1 can't answer the question, it moves to C-1, and then D-1 (or other groups). If no one can answer, A-1 answers and A-2 asks the next question of B-2, C-2, and so on. If B-2 answers the question satisfactorily, he or she asks C-2 (D-2, etc.) the first question from Group B's list. This activity should move quickly and involve all the class members.

Advantages: Students get practice in asking questions and in active participation. The teacher should also participate in this activity (students love to stump the teacher).

Variations:

1. Have the groups concoct questions for ten minutes. Write all of the questions on the board or a flip chart. Have each group select a different question to discuss (one for each group). Each group then discusses its question for fifteen minutes. Afterwards, the group leaders present brief summaries to the class.

2. Same as above, except give Group A's questions to Group B, Group B's to C, etc.

Assessment:

1. Students keep questions in their portfolio. They can identify the types of questions by marking them: Open = +, Closed = C, Unanswered = ?, Opinion-centered = O, Factual = #.

2. Each group member writes a paragraph summary of the findings. They exchange these summaries with a partner who: (1) Agrees, disagrees, adds to with a brief statement, and (2) Adds another question that needs to be answered.

Reasoning Exercise 3: Pairing Partners for Review

Objective: To give students the opportunity to verbalize a topic, to analyze details, and to synthesize.

Approach: Divide the class into pairs. Assign sections of literature under study to each pair. Ask students to select a scene and record the page(s). Their task is to design two or three questions for another pair's response, such as: (1) select a phrase and explain its relationship to the plot; (2) find phrases that explain how the character felt at that moment or what his or her relationship is to other characters; or (3) compare this scene with another in the same or different literary text. Next they write answers to their own questions.

Then the pairs exchange questions. Each pair discusses the possible answers and writes a single response. Afterwards, each group of four (two pairs) should meet and discuss the questions and answers. The four can then decide which one or two questions should be presented to the entire class for an oral response.

Advantages: Students discuss elements of the literature. They must also evaluate responses and relate those responses to their previous knowledge.

Variations:

1. Pairs can present one of their questions to the class orally. This way they receive immediate feedback and more oral practice.

2. One set of pairs can discuss their questions and answers in a fish bowl, while the rest of the class listens and evaluates the accuracy and depth of their responses. (In the fish bowl, one group sits in the center of the larger group and discusses as though alone. The purpose of this method is to practice the skills of discussion and get feedback from nonparticipants.)

Assessment:

1. Check the pair's questions, answers, and evaluations of the other pair's responses for completeness and accuracy.

2. Photocopy the pair's questions and responses so that each person has a copy.

3. Give students oral feedback based on the interactions.

Reasoning Exercise 4: Group Debate

Objective: To use the skills of argument by presenting key ideas and supports and listening to recognize others' arguments. Students should fashion questions for clarification and to probe for more information. They should analyze the accuracy of cause-and-effect reasoning, and the nature of problems and solutions.

Approach: Select one or two issues about which students have some prior knowledge from class, home, or the media. Suggested topics include welfare reform, affirmative action, sexual harassment, capital punishment, the UN, drunk driving, child abuse, animal cruelty, environmental preservation, and literary questions.

Divide the class in half. One side will speak affirmatively and the other side negatively on a proposition, such as:

Resolved: Persons who are mentally retarded should not be held responsible for the crimes they commit. (*Of Mice and Men*, John Steinbeck)

Resolved: Parents and guardians found guilty of child abuse should be prosecuted to the full extent of the law. (*The Color Purple*, Alice Walker)

Resolved: Divorce laws should be made more strict. (*A Doll's House*, Henrik Ibsen)

Resolved: Individuals should have the right to end their lives. (*The Heart of the Matter*, Graham Greene)

Allow ten minutes for the students to write down opinions on the subject. During this writing period, they should independently record ideas, questions, and the reasons they favor or oppose the resolution, and at this point, there should be no talking.

Next have groups choose, or appoint, a chairperson for each team. The chairperson should be someone who will listen fairly to all remarks. Form two circles. Each person in turn states *one* idea. The chairperson records the comments by placing them in columns headed "Affirmative Arguments" or "Negative Arguments." Both categories are helpful, since to win a debate one must know what one's opponents will argue and be prepared to refute those arguments. After the first round of comments, the students should continue sharing single ideas until all have been stated.

Next, direct the teams to rank the arguments on their side of the proposition from least important to most important. At this time, they should try to think of one reason to support each idea. They also should try to develop answers to the opposition's possible arguments. The chairperson records the counterarguments. When the team's plans are complete, the chairperson reviews aloud the notes he or she has made. Then the students decide in which order and on what point they will speak. The last person to speak should be the chairperson, or the strongest speaker, since his or her job is to summarize the best and winning arguments from preceding speeches.

When the teams are prepared, begin the debate. The following order of events is suggested: The first affirmative speaker brings up the least important argument and explains it for one minute. The negative team then questions the speaker for the same amount of time. Next, the first negative speaker refutes the affirmative argument, followed by the affirmative team questioning the speaker for one minute. Each speaker from alternating sides then takes the floor for a minute, trying to answer the previous arguments and adding or extending his or her own side's position. The last speaker on each side concludes the debate with a speech that refutes the opposition and restates his or her group's case.

If it is necessary to lengthen the times for speeches or questioning, make sure both sides are equalized. The final speeches should be twice as long as the preliminary speeches, whatever their length. Have the students move their desks so they face the opposing side, then each student can speak from his or her desk, if they decide not to use the "speaker's lectern" in the front of the room.

Advantages: Group debate allows students to explore causal relationships and problem solving. It also stimulates the classification of ideas. The immediate feedback permits students to modify their ideas in relation to challenging information. The focus should be on the group's position, rather than allowing one or two students to "carry" the debate.

Variations:

1. Divide the class into fourths. You can select two topics or just use the one.

2. To provide practice in research, have students use information technology (IT) and print resources to find supporting evidence for both the pro and con positions on topics. Each student could prepare three cards that list a source and evidence from the source. The group members would then pool their data, organize arguments, and proceed as in the usual group debate.

Assessment:

1. Group assessment: Note the arguments each group presents. Record the supports they use for their arguments. What questions do they ask the opposing side? Notice the kinds of responses they give when challenged or questioned. Do they answer the opposing side in the final argument? Give a summary of your observations immediately following the debate, without declaring a winner. Tape the debate if possible.

2. Have a student keep a tally of how often each individual speaks or questions.

3. Write a group review and distribute copies to each member.

4. If you use four groups, the two not debating can critique the ones who are.

Reasoning Exercise 5: Student Congress

Objective: To develop skill in problem solving and to develop an understanding of cause and effect and comparison and contrast.

Approach: Generate a list of topics that reflect issues of interest to the students. Divide the class into groups. Each group selects a topic for debate. The groups research the topics to learn the major problems with the current policies. Then as a group they write a bill about social, political, or economic issues. The suggested topics from Reasoning Exercise 4: Group Debate can be used. In addition, students can debate such topics as genetic research or space exploration. (These particular subjects lend themselves to a science fiction unit.)

A bill may be simply stated: "Be It Enacted That: Genetic research will not be limited by governmental restrictions."

When all of the groups have generated a bill with a portfolio of supporting information, set an agenda. Students should be given copies of the other bills and a chance to research these topics as well. This assignment is an excellent opportunity to utilize information technology (IT). Direct them to a Web search engine. Some of the more popular search engines are: Alta Vista (*www.altavista:digital.com*), Excite (*www.excite.com*), and HotBot (*www.hotbot.com*). Directories are subject catalogs of various web resources. Some are evaluated and filtered. Three powerful ones are: Yahoo (*www.yahoo.com*), Dig (*www.digdisney.com*), and Education World (*www.education-world.com*). If you want to be sure your information is reliable use an Online Encyclopedia like Funk and Wagnall's Knowledge Center (*www.funkandwagnalls.com*) or Education World (*www.education-world.com*).

The goal is to deliver two speeches, the first in favor of their own bill, the second for or against one of the other bills. Appoint a presiding officer to oversee the proceedings. Parliamentary procedures can be handled effectively by students with a simplified format. The National Forensic League has developed a modified chart of rules for the most frequently used parliamentary motions (See Figure 3–2).

On the day of the congress, the author of the first bill speaks in favor of his or her legislation. A questioning period of two minutes follows. All members of the "house" participate. It is the presiding officer's job to allow only one question at a time. After the questioning period, debate continues with alternating negative and affirmative speeches of about one minute's length, with a minute of questioning for each speaker. When all the necessary information has been deliberated, a member "calls the question" and the house votes to pass or fail the legislation.

Advantages: Students get an in-depth look at the underlying causes of important social, political, or economic problems. "Group" work helps them practice ideas and deal with the hurdle of challenging other people's ideas in a public forum. They can change or modify opinions in the course of the debate—in fact, such changes reflect "desired outcomes" of discussions in the Student Congress format. Students gain an understanding of how our government works.

Figure 3–2
Table of Most Frequently Used Parliamentary Motions*

Type	Motion	Purpose	Second Required?	Debatable?	Amendable?	Required Vote
Privileged	24. Fix Time for Reassembling	To arrange time of next meeting	Yes	Yes-T	Yes-T	Majority
	23. Adjourn	To dismiss the meeting	Yes	No	Yes-T	Majority
	22. To Recess	To dismiss the meeting for a specific length of time	Yes	Yes	Yes-T	Majority
	21. Rise to a Question of Privilege	To make a personal request during debate	No	No	No	Decision of Chair
	20. Call for the Orders of the Day	To force consideration of a postponed motion	No	No	No	Decision of Chair
Incidental	19. Appeal a Decision of the Chair	To reverse the decision of the chairman	Yes	No	No	Majority
	18. Rise to a Point of Order or Parliamentary Procedure	To correct a parliamentary error or ask a question	No	No	No	Decision of Chair
	17. To Call for a Roll Call Vote	To verify a voice vote	Yes	No	No	1/5
	16. Object to the Consideration of a Question	To suppress action	No	No	No	2/3
	15. To Divide a Motion	To consider its parts separately	Yes	No	Yes	Majority
	14. Leave to Modify or Withdraw a Motion	To modify or withdraw a motion	No	No	No	Majority
	13. To Suspend the Rules	To take action contrary to standing rules	Yes	No	No	2/3
Subsidiary	12. To Rescind	To repeal previous action	Yes	Yes	Yes	2/3
	11. To Reconsider	To consider a defeated motion again	Yes	Yes	No	Majority
	10. To take from the Table	To consider tabled motion	Yes	No	No	Majority
	9. To Lay on the Table	To defer action	Yes	No	No	Majority
	8. Previous Question	To force an immediate vote	Yes	No	No	2/3
	7. To Limit or Extend Debate	To modify freedom of debate	Yes	Yes	Yes-T	2/3
	6. To Postpone to a Certain Time	To defer action	Yes	Yes	Yes	Majority
	5. To Refer to a Committee*	For further study	Yes	Yes	Yes	Majority
	4. To Amend an Amendment*	To modify an amendment	1/3	Yes	No	Majority
	3. To Amend*	To modify a motion	1/3	Yes	Yes	Majority
	2. To Postpone Indefinitely	To suppress action	Yes	Yes	No	Majority
Main	1. Main Motion	To introduce a business	Yes	Yes	Yes	Majority

*National Forensic League Student Congress Manual, 1990, p. SCM-5. Reprinted with permission from the National Forensic League. [May be photocopied for classroom use even though not specified.]

Variation: Student Congress can be used to review a work of literature. For the play *Pygmalion* by George Bernard Shaw, for instance, the bill debated could be the following: "Be It Enacted That: No person shall be discriminated against on account of language, dialect, or speech." Students could explore the issues around the use of English versus other languages, a current "hot" topic in some areas of the country.

Assessment: Since this project has many components, assessment is based on a variety of items.

1. The group portfolio of resources
2. Individual speeches
3. Participation in the congress
4. Knowledge of Parliamentary procedures
5. Leadership roles (group, presiding officer)
6. Group effort

Reasoning Exercise 6: Modified Lincoln-Douglas Debate

Objective: To introduce students to logical analysis through formal refutation techniques. In this exercise, students must support propositions with logic, evidence, and examples.

Approach: Divide the class into four groups. Give each group a value proposition. These statements can relate to issues of general concern, literature, or both.

"Civil disobedience is justified in a democracy." *Walden,* Henry David Thoreau

"Hamlet's treatment of Ophelia is merited." *Hamlet,* William Shakespeare

"Protecting the environment is more important than economic progress."*Animal Dreams,* Barbara Kingsolver

"It is not possible to be ethical in American business."*All My Sons,* Arthur Miller

Half of each group is affirmative, the other half negative. Students construct arguments supporting their position using theories, examples, and facts. These arguments are presented in three-minute speeches.

The following order of events is suggested: A group member holding the affirmative position presents a constructive speech. A member holding the negative position cross-examines that speaker. The negative side then presents a constructive speech that refutes the affirmative position and builds an alternative argument. A member of the affirmative side cross-examines the negative speaker. The next affirmative speaker rebuts that position to rebuild the affirmative case. The negative side responds with their own rebuttal. The debate ends with a one-minute speech by the affirmative side. This format takes about twenty minutes; therefore, it is possible to have about two debates in a class period. While one group presents their debate, the other class members take notes. They can then critique the debate, declare the winners, and give reasons for their decision. A paragraph justifying the decision allows the teacher to discover how well the students were listening.

The following times are suggested for affirmative and negative speeches:

Affirmative Constructive	3 Minutes
Negative Cross-Examination	2 Minutes
Negative Constructive	3 Minutes
Affirmative Cross-Examination	2 Minutes
Affirmative Rebuttal	2 Minutes
Negative Rebuttal	3 Minutes
Affirmative Rebuttal	1 Minute

Advantages: Students learn to recognize cause-and-effect factors, underlying principles, and logical connections. They also learn more effective listening skills.

Variations:

1. Alter the time format.
2. Allow for questioning time after the first two rebuttal speeches.
3. Divide the class into groups of four. Assign two students to the affirmative side of the proposition and two to the negative. One student on each side does the constructive portion of the debate, while his or her partner does the rebuttal. Partners may consult with each other between speeches.

Assessment:

1. Peer critiques evaluate the strength of arguments.
2. The paragraphs justifying the decisions are evaluations of the debaters' understanding of the issues and argument structure.
3. The teacher can give oral feedback about the process and suggest ways to improve debate.

Predicting

Recognizing alternative courses of action and determining what consequences may result from behaviors and events involves a level of abstraction called "predicting." Moving mentally beyond the observable present to a future or past time in order to understand situations better also requires advanced abstraction skills. These skills of prediction can be fostered through drama-related exercises because the interpretation of character demands recognizing subtleties and responding to them, often in an unconscious manner. Successful interpretation is a tangible inferential thinking experience. Only through inference can one convey the author's meaning to others. Various types of dramatic activities are used in the predicting exercises, including role playing and readers theatre.

Role Playing

Drama gives students a chance to play out life. John McCreesh describes the value of drama as the opportunity to "absorb and communicate experience . . . Through drama the child can be encouraged to play out a variety of emotional experiences, and undergo many imaginative experiences" (1977, 118). Both scripted and unscripted exercises may be used. Unscripted drama exercises allow students not only to view past emotions but also to encounter new feelings in a safe way.

Assumed fictitious roles suggest dialogue that will become part of the students' internalized speech. I witnessed a good example of this in a U.K. classroom where the children could not learn some standard grammatical constructions. However, when they role-played "society" people, they naturally spoke faultless English. Drama allows students to vary thought patterns without paying the price of reality. In addition, it does not take a drama specialist to use improvisation, role playing, and student-written scripts. For the purpose of developing predicting skills, polished acting is less important than dramatic imagination. The process is the goal, not performance for an audience.

For the process to work, a climate of trust is essential, since both the teacher and the students fear appearing foolish. Encouragement is a must. Give only positive suggestions, and keep criticism to a minimum. Most of the exercises in this book require that the students first place themselves in the roles of the characters through writing. From there, they can move to more sophisticated tasks such as character interviews or conversations. As they develop their characters, they can elaborate on new situations and relations for their assumed personalities.

Role playing between two characters helps to determine motivations. After students have written a monologue as Macbeth or Lady Macbeth and read it aloud to their small group or the class, you can assign a scene to a pair of Macbeths or Lady Macbeths. For example, "Lady Macbeth, suspecting Macbeth's intention to harm Lady Macduff, approaches her husband to find out his intention." Have several pairs enact the same scene. This allows for more lively discussion, challenges, and interpretations. Insights into human motivation develop quickly after students have walked in various characters' shoes for awhile. It is possible, then, for students to hypothesize about possible future events that these characters might appear in, to forecast future behaviors, and to construct alternate circumstances. Drama activities thus promote higher levels of abstraction.

Readers Theatre

Readers theatre, a type of oral interpretation of literature, is similar to role playing but is slightly different in purpose and performance. The first major difference is that it is scripted. The second difference is that although acting and oral interpretation have elements in common, acting requires that the performer *become* the character he or she is portraying. Oral interpretation, on the other hand, requires that the performer *suggest* the character or characters. The fictitious people and setting exist only in the imagination of the reader and the audience. Interpretative readers must therefore employ their imagination to accomplish this feat. They must feel the characters' emotions so completely that their voices and bodies create mental images for the audience.

Some procedures can assist in developing this inferential thinking. Students should become totally familiar with the text, studying both the connotation and denotation of the words. They must also ask themselves questions: Who is this character? What might he eat for breakfast? How did he get along with his father and mother? What time of day is it? What is the setting? What is the author trying to say? Short informal writings on questions like these help to focus feelings.

The highest level of synthesis occurs when the student masters interpretation, because it demands combining all the parts within a work and presenting them as a unified whole. The reader *becomes* the intrinsic meaning through the vehicle of the performance.

Predicting Exercises

The six exercises in this section are designed to promote students' ability in such predicting-related skills as making inferences, hypothesizing, and forecasting. They can be applied toward Standard 4 (40): *"Students effectively use speaking and listening skills to create meaning, develop ideas, and make decisions."*

Predicting Exercise 1: Become-a-Character

Objective: To experience a literary or historical event through interpretation of a character or historical personage. Through this experience, students learn to make inferences about motives, personalities, and events.

Approach: Divide the class into four groups. The task of each group is to "become" a character. First the group members study the information available about the character. Next, they write a ten-minute narrative in the persona of the character. This narrative should pertain to a dramatic situation (for example, the discovery of a betrayal, signing the Declaration of Independence, or planning to murder another character), and can be a diary entry, a letter, or a monologue.

Following the writing, which should "set" the character, the group discusses the situation, maintaining their assigned role. This discussion is not role playing in the traditional sense of "acting out" a part. Rather, it is "thinking out" a part to create a metaphor. The traditional end-of-chapter questions can be answered with the students still in character. This approach heightens discussion and interest.

Sample: (To be used after Act I of *Julius Caesar.*) The characters are Caesar, Brutus, Cassius, and Casca. Each group rereads all of their character's parts aloud, noticing not only what the character says and does, but also what others say about and to him. This preparation should take about twenty minutes.

Next, each group is given a writing assignment. The time limit is ten minutes, and the goal is to write two pages. The assignments are the following:

You are Caesar:

You are Brutus:

You are Cassius:

You are Casca:

Students devote the next part of the class period to assuming the roles they created when discussing Act I. They sit in a large circle with all the Caesars in one section, the Brutuses in another, and so forth for the other characters. Beginning with Caesar, each student reads or tells his thoughts. At this point, those who are Brutus or another character may ask Caesar questions. More than one answer may be given to a particular question, depending on the character's viewpoint. For instance, when Brutus asks Caesar if he plans to accept the crown and become emperor, one of the Caesars may deny this ambition, while another may be eager to rule. Eventually, it becomes clear that Caesar is a multifaceted personality. Other characters are similarly interviewed and allowed to reveal their thoughts.

It is important when structuring this type of exercise to complete the cycle in one class period, because a mood and momentum develop, and it is hard to recapture them on a second day.

Advantages: Students experience inferential thinking and learn to make connections between character motivation and plot. They also gain a greater understanding of the author's skill.

Variations:

Talk to Antony in private about your past successes, future plans, and concerns. (Write a monologue, not a conversation.)

Write a letter to Claudius, a Roman friend who is visiting in Spain, about your concerns for Rome.

You are in a meeting with some key conspirators. Give a speech about your plans to take care of the "Caesar situation."

You have gone to Paulus, a senator, after leaving Cassius the night before the Ides of March to convince him to join the conspirators. In a monologue, tell him all the reasons you can think of that he should become a part of the plot.

Become-an-Author: Have students assume the persona of the author of a book they have read. A single "author" or a panel of "authors" can then be interviewed by "experts" in the field of literature in a mock TV show. Questions can range from "What influenced you to select the setting of your book?" to "Did anything from your life cause you to write this book?"

Assessment:

1. The character groups should summarize the findings about their character. These summaries can be evaluated for the level of understanding regarding the characters and their situation.

2. Keep a record of the behaviors that listeners use to clarify speakers' messages.

Predicting Exercise 2: Character Interviews

Objective: To create a situation that promotes inferential thinking and to foster hypotheses about existing or future problems.

Approach: Using the techniques of "Become-a-Character," divide students into several "character" groups and one "author" or "reporter" group. Again, students are to write for ten minutes in their assumed roles. The author or reporter writes about how he or she sees the characters and/or the situations. Then, the various participants think of questions they would like to ask other characters or author/reporter.

Set up the classroom with the author/reporter group in the front of the room. Have the rest of the characters sit in a semicircle so that they can see and interact with each other. Groups take turns asking questions and answering. Students must observe two main rules: (1) All answers must be given in character. (2) All participants must speak.

Advantages: By responding in an unaccustomed persona, students extend their ability to decenter their thinking and thus extend their ability to abstract.

Variations:

1. Have each group divide into characters with one person taking the role of reporter or author. In a panel format, the characters explain who they are and are questioned by the author or reporter. Members of the audience also have a chance to question them.

2. Use pairs. One is the biographer. The other is one of the characters. After the biographer interviews the character, he or she introduces the character to the audience. The character responds to questions by the audience.

Assessment:

1. Make audio- or videotapes of the character interactions. Play back for the class. Listen to evaluate the accuracy of the information about the characters or the book.

2. Have the groups draw pictures of their characters and write brief descriptions. Display these in the hall or cafeteria. They can present this information to other audiences.

Predicting Exercise 3: Character Conversations

Objective: To stimulate the ability to forecast what kinds of motives or actions a set of circumstances will produce.

Approach: Using the steps in "Become-a-Character," establish four or five character groups. Then create a problem for two or more of the characters to solve. For example, "Lady Macbeth, suspecting that Macbeth means to harm Banquo, detains Banquo at the castle. Macbeth enters. What happens?" Begin the problem solving by choosing an individual "Banquo" and "Lady Macbeth" to role-play the scene. Change the person playing Banquo at mid-scene or at a convenient point. This switch allows for a new interpretation. The scene can be played again with different individuals and a different outcome.

Next, present another problem involving the same characters. For example: "The banquet scene: The ghost of Banquo can speak. He is seen by Lady Macbeth as well as Macbeth. What happens?" (Students can also think up "What if . . ." situations.)

Advantages: Students increase their ability to extend interpretation. When more than one person is involved in a role, empathy for that role increases, as does the variation in interpretation.

Variation: Give one group the job of creating situations and "directing" the characters.

Assessment:

1. Students write self-assessments of what they learned through playing the scene and what questions remain.

2. Observers write assessments about the accuracy of the portrayals, effective character elements, and suggestions for improving the scenes.

Predicting Exercise 4: Readers Theatre

Objective: To translate meaning from one form into another. This involves the skills of inferring, hypothesizing, and forecasting. Students must visualize concepts and communicate the meaning of those concepts to an audience. In this activity, both the process and the product are important.

Approach: Divide the students into groups of four or five. Assign them short works of prose, poetry, drama, or historical incidents involving personalities. Students may then change the texts into original scripts or select segments for dramatic readings. The time limit for performance should be about fifteen minutes. All of the previous exercises are helpful in preparing students for this drama-like activity.

Readers theatre has no set rules. Students may wear costumes, but the action is continuous; therefore, they should suggest characters rather than "become" them. Sometimes, a scarf or a hat may be enough to suggest a character. Props can be used, but they are not necessary. Readers may sit, stand, or lie. They can move about or remain stationary. Music, lighting effects, backdrops, and scenery are all possibilities. Narrators, in character, can be used to explain the purpose or to eclipse the time frame. Practical suggestions for oral interpretation and readers theatre can be found in Randall McCutcheon, James Schaffer, and Joseph R. Wycoff's book, *Communication Matters* (1994).

A variety of novels, plays, short stories, and poetry can be presented to a class vividly and with meaning when the teacher wants to survey a genre or period. Students can research famous personalities or events and present them to the class with biographical sketches, scenes, and portions of documents. The result is a "collage" effect which makes the subject matter more striking *and* palatable.

Advantages: Students share meaning and interpretation, and the discussion of techniques encourages thinking about interpretations. For example, the choice of whether to wear costumes or use musical background forces students to consider the meaning of the text.

Variation: Students can write original monologues, poetry, or scripts about a literary work or historical event and present as above.

Assessment:

1. Listeners critique the way readers use their voices and bodies to convey meaning.
2. Pairs of critiquers evaluate how the selection and organization of materials make a comprehensive statement.
3. The groups prepare feedback forms for listeners to complete regarding the performance.
4. After all the groups have presented their interpretations, discuss how well criteria were met and set up guidelines for future performances.

Predicting Exercise 5: Old-Time Radio

Objective: To practice informative listening, noting details, making associations, relating parts to a whole.

Approach: Students listen to a story from an old-time radio broadcast (available on casette) and take notes on different elements that contribute to the impact of the story. Suggested topics: sound effects, the setting (time period, time of day, location, weather), major features of the character(s), plot incidents. Before the climax, stop the tape and ask the students to write their prediction of the ending. Finish playing the tape. Discuss what the listeners noted about each of the areas and how the ending corresponded to their prediction. They can compare images that came to their minds and how radio differs from TV or film.

Variations:

1. Students draw a sketch of a scene or the character and explain why they "saw" it that particular way.
2. Students make audiotapes of their own scripts and listeners take note of the various elements.

Assessment:

1. Listen to an assortment of radio broadcasts and repeat process. Keep a record of the quantity and quality of observations made by individuals.
2. Have groups listen to a tape, compare notes, and present a report of their findings.

Predicting Exercise 6: Script Writing/Performing

Objective: To write an original script that demonstrates an understanding of the way oral communication reveals characters' feelings and personality.

Approach: Divide the class into pairs. If the number is uneven, use one group of three. Hand out the description of the project shown in Figure 3–3.

Variations:

1. The performance can be recorded on audio- and videotape.

2. Individuals can write scripts first. Then work with a partner to perform both scripts.

3. Scenes from a book can be scripted into the students' own language.

Assessment:

1. The performance can be evaluated on preestablished criteria: originality, character dynamics, realistic dialogue, and believable emotional development.

2. Listeners describe their perception of character development and how the conversation revealed the feelings and relationships.

3. If tapes are made, they can become part of the assessment portfolio.

Projecting

Learning to project is more difficult than learning to predict. Projecting requires implicit analysis and synthesis, paralleling the highest cognitive levels in Bloom's (1979) hierarchy of thinking skills. Bloom's classification is limited, however, if we are to assume that mere recognition of parts and their relationship to a whole is the most challenging type of thought. Even projecting ideas into new circumstances does not encompass the most complex form of abstraction, synectic thinking. This level of thinking is more subtle, harder to define, and correspondingly more difficult to teach. Yet, it seems possible to create a climate that allows this kind of thought to happen in a classroom. Intuition, poetry, and language play are all relevant to the creation of such a climate.

Figure 3–3
Creating a Dramatic Dialogue

Objective: Write a script using a dialogue between two or three persons.

Method: Prepare a script with the following restrictions:

1. Use a single setting.

2. Plot a single uninterrupted scene. The playing time of the script will be the same as the length of time the action takes in the script. (10 minutes maximum)

3. Stage directions should contain only what can be seen and heard. (Do not include background information, off-stage happenings, or descriptions of thoughts or feelings.)

4. Use dialogue to reveal character, background information, feelings of characters.

5. Title your script.

Practice the script until you know it. (Write the parts on three-by-five-inch cards so that the pages of a script are not distracting.)

Perform the dialogue for the class.

*****

Possible Situations:

1. A parent and child conflict about rules.

2. An unexpected visitor arrives.

3. A student tries to explain an unexcused absence to the teacher.

4. An unpleasant neighbor calls with another complaint.

5. Two friends with different ideas about a good time try to plan an outing.

6. Two astronauts exploring an unknown planet make a discovery.

7. The baby-sitter tries to cope with the neighborhood pest.

8. A nervous applicant interviews for a job.

9. Two people at a cafeteria lunch table have a dispute.

10. A friend shows up who owes money.

Intuition and Poetry

Synectic thinking is the concept that two or more unrelated elements join to form something entirely new, placing this kind of thought at a level of abstraction beyond synthesis. The added ingredients are intuition, feeling, and metaphor. Synectics is "an operational theory for the conscious use of the preconscious psychological mechanisms present in . . . creative activity"(Gordon 1961, 3). Less formally stated, synectics is a process we employ in relating to experience and in making meaning for ourselves—if only on a subconscious level.

Each individual creates in his or her own way, through a perception of events, a uniquely personal world. The whole of that personal world is created imaginatively, capitalizing on reconciliation of seemingly dissimilar elements. As human beings, we must move past logic to solve the great conflicts of our existence. James Britton notes some of these "irreconcilable demands" (1982a, 27) in his essay "Poetry and Our Pattern of Culture." Our need to conform wars with the desire to rebel. Our need to be adventurous wars with the need for security. The need to love is at odds with the law of the jungle. Such conflicts require supralogical reconciliation and explain the need for art, literature, and music.

Poetry, as an example of metaphorical thinking, is ideally suited to achieve a resolution of opposites. Born of tension within the artist, it expresses conflicting and contrasting forces with words, emotion, and rhythm. When poetry achieves a unity, we say it works well.

Britton refers to the "many-sidedness" of life situations, and especially to a "two-sidedness" or "polarity," with which poetry can deal more effectively than prose (1982a, 28):

> The language of poetry, it seems to me, differs most from the language of prose statement in the power it possesses to represent, indeed to recreate, this two-sidedness. It does so in many ways—by its ambiguous use of words and syntax, by using rhythm and the corporeal qualities of words to give a sense that may be at variance with the paraphrasable meaning; by using images which may themselves bring contrary impulses into play.

The poem creates a response in the reader by tapping the common intuitional bond that exists among all human beings. Emotion is the psychological reality that dictates our responses to facts. The force of emotion is the power that helps us "see" truth as accurately as the electron microscope enables biologists to study cells. It is feeling that penetrates experience and allows us to travel the involuted path to understanding. The poet uses all the resources of words to achieve this kind of insight. True critical thinking must employ similar mind-search techniques to uncover hidden meanings about our universe.

Those mysteries can sometimes be discovered through metaphors. Aristotle, who defined the metaphor, held that mastering the technique is a sign of genius and as such cannot be learned (Gibbs 1995). We may not all have the swift vision of an Emily Dickinson who perceives "The Brain is just the weight of God" (1981, 845), however we can tap this powerful mind resource. If we deliberately juxtapose two dissimilar ideas, we can make startling connections. The mind is a storehouse of impressions, and when stimulated, oddly correct insights may occur.

We learn only from the *interpretation* of experience. Mathematicians who can play with symbols, create analogies, derive theorems, and experiment with permutations are the ones who will solve the world's great riddles. We need engineers and scientists, not just poets, who can employ intuitive thought and play with ideas.

Language Play

The projecting exercises that follow are designed to assist metaphoric response and to contribute to the expressive use of language. They consist primarily of language play. While the word *play* connotes frivolity, the antithesis of most people's view of critical thinking, the opposite is true. Play, fantasizing, and creativity are high levels of abstraction. As envisioned by Donald Winnicott in his book *Playing and Reality* (1971), play is an area of free activity lying between the inner personal reality and the outer environment. This "third area" is essential for the creative life to expand. It is part of all artistic creation. Play allows us to suspend reality and our own concerns temporarily in order to experiment with new juxtapositions and combinations.

James Britton suggests that "the arts (including literature) represent a highly organized activity within the general area of play" (1982b, 42). This "art-like" organization functions in a different way from cognitive organization. *How* this is so is not clear, nor is why. What we do know is that the need for this type of thought is real. Higher mathematics and science are as much artistic endeavors as are sociological and philosophical thought. The more abstract the realm, the more blurred the delineation between the cognitive and the creative. Teachers should thus strive to create a space in which the "third area" can live.

Projecting Exercises

The six exercises in this section promote the skill of projecting by involving students in various aspects of this kind of thought. They actively seek intuitive responses, project into the feelings of others, manipulate ideas, and penetrate the deeper meaning of words and ideas.

These activities are ways to build the skills required for Standard 3 (40): "*Students understand and critically respond to print, nonprint, media, and information technology (IT) sources.*"

Projecting Exercise 1: How a Poem Acts

Objective: To project the feelings and experiences a poem evokes through a dramatic performance. To achieve this, students must understand the connotations of words.

Approach: Select poems that have some movement, sounds, or emotions. Good poems for this exercise are "At Grass," by Philip Larkin; "The Thought-Fox," by Ted Hughes; "The Animals' Arrival," by Elizabeth Jennings; "Refugee Blues," by W. H. Auden; and "The Summer Day" by Mary Oliver.

Divide the class into groups of four or five students. Give a different poem to each group, with enough copies so that every member will have one. Each group is to plan a dramatic presentation of the poem with each member taking an active part. There are no rules about how the presentation should be performed. To prepare for their presentation, each group should complete the following in fifteen minutes:

1. Read the poem aloud once or twice.
2. Listen to the sounds as well as for the meaning.
3. Think about sound effects that would enhance a presentation of the poem—wind blowing, a clock ticking, the ocean's roar, etc.
4. Think what kinds of voices should read different parts.
5. Decide which parts can be read solo and which can be read in chorus.
6. Decide how group members will sit, stand, or lie in the presentation.
7. Think of gestures or other movements that will dramatize the poem's effect.
8. Practice the poem once or twice.
9. Return to the large group to perform.

After their presentation, ask students to respond to two questions:

1. What was most useful to you in preparing your dramatic performance?
2. What, if anything, hindered your performance?

Discussion should follow, with groups asking each other questions about the interpretations. It is helpful to have repeat performances after the discussion.

Advantage: Listening to rhythm and "feeling" poetry enhances understanding for both performers and listeners.

Variations:

1. Several poems by one author can be presented to show similarities or contrasts in style.
2. Original poetry can be performed.

Assessment:

1. Ask class members to determine the performing group's understanding of the poem's meaning as conveyed through their presentation.
2. Members of the group write pre-performance and post-performance journals about their understanding of the poetry they performed.
3. Videotape the performance for review.

Projecting Exercise 2: What a Poem Says

Objective: To freely associate words and meanings in a poem, building intuitive responses to words and images.

Approach: This activity should follow Projecting Exercise 1, "How a Poem Acts." Suggested poems include "The Send-Off," by Wilfred Owen; "Embassy," by W. H. Auden; "Evans," by R. S. Thomas; "A Refusal to Mourn the Death, by Fire, of a Child in London," by Dylan Thomas; "Hully Gully" by Rita Dove; "the earth is a living thing" by Lucille Clifton.

Divide the class into groups of four or five. Give each group copies of a different poem. The task is to discover what the poem is saying and how. Allow ten minutes for group discussion. Emphasize that there are no "correct" answers; the students will simply be readers responding to language. The group members should use the following format for discussion:

1. Read the poem aloud once or twice with different readers taking different parts.
2. Discuss the following questions. (Group members may write individual answers first, then share with the group.)
   A. What kinds of sounds do you hear?
   B. How would you stage this poem?

   C. What memories or experiences of your own are brought to mind?

   D. Are there any parts you don't understand? What would help to clarify these parts?

   E. Who is the speaker of the poem?

   F. What images are most vivid or meaningful to you?

After discussion, the small groups return to the large group and read their poems aloud, using skills of oral interpretation. After presenting their poem, each group explains its meaning to the class and what emotions/memories it evoked. Again, this is an open-ended discussion with no "right answer" tag line.

Advantages: This exercise is a more cognitive approach to poetry than "How a Poem Acts." It provides another way to "get into" a poem, and it increases students' ability to create new meanings.

Variation:

Create-a-Project: Groups can devise a project for another group to carry out for the poem, for example, creating a game, a movie script, a play, a painting, or a tableau. The groups can then discuss and practice their assigned projects, return to class, and give a presentation.

Assessment:

   1. Group members ask the listeners to answer the same questions they addressed in preparation to learn alternative reactions.

   2. Individuals make a collection of poems. For each they write a reaction similar to the one they made in collaboration with the group.

Projecting Exercise 3: Own-a-Word

Objective: To foster an awareness of the connotations of words as well as their denotations. This exercise stimulates metaphoric thinking. "Own-a-Word" helps students to manipulate ideas; therefore, it is particularly useful for difficult terms.

Approach: Give each student a word to "own." The student's task is to present the word to the class in a unique, distinctly individual way. In the student's hands, the word may become a poster, an acrostic poem, a story, a pet that needs special treatment, or a weapon. Part of the assignment is to produce a *visual image* of the word. These images can be gathered in a booklet, posted on a bulletin board, or used to decorate the hall outside the classroom.

Individuals present their words orally, explaining what they did and why. Years later my students still remembered "their" words. For example, one sophomore wrote this acrostic for *pacifist:*

Peace-loving
Afraid
Civilian
Immune to hate
Friendly to everyone
Interested in a perfect world
Spiteful of war
Too trustful

Advantages: Playing with words helps to make them the students' own. They are also able to see the unique possibilities a word contains.

Variations:

1. **Sell-a-Word:** Have students compose short persuasive speeches about why others should buy their word. They should explain the word's special uses, features, values, and why their particular word is needed by the general public. This assignment can be videotaped as a TV commercial, or audiotaped as a radio commercial.

2. Groups of students can work on the "Own-a-Word" project with multiple terms or words. They can devise skits, costumes, and posters.

Assessment:

1. Students receive credit for using the words imaginatively in other assignments.

2. Students write metaphoric poetry for their words. These can be collected and become part of the poetry portfolio.

Projecting Exercise 4: Metaphoric Questions

Objective: To encourage the manipulation of ideas by placing them into different contexts.

Approach: After the class has completed a unit of work, divide them into groups of four or five. Provide each group with several metaphoric questions (as suggested below). They select one or several and generate as many responses as possible in fifteen minutes. The advantage of working with metaphoric questions is that they challenge the mind to clarify issues and points of contention. In addition, they bring into focus unperceived relationships and unify concepts. Group evolvement of ideas can lead to students making similar intuitive leaps on their own after practice.

The following are samples of metaphoric questions. Insert whatever topic is being studied in the blanks.

1. Describe _____ as a product advertised on TV. What kind of company would sell it? What actor would promote it? What age group would buy it? What kind of show does the product sponsor? What are the product's benefits?

2. Describe _____ as a TV show. Who would star in it? Would the reruns be popular? What time of day would it air? What are the chances of the program being serialized or imitated by others?

3. Describe _____ as a place. Who would visit it? Would it be written up in travel brochures? What kind of wardrobe would a traveler need who visits there? Would it have many inhabitants? What kind of government, economy, and language would the place have?

4. Describe _____ as an animal. What is its habitat? What are its natural enemies? What is its diet? Would the animal live better in captivity or in the wild?

5. Describe _____ as a musical piece. What style of music is it? Who would perform it? What kinds of audiences would it attract? Who would promote it? How well would its CDs sell?

6. Describe _____ as an object. Where is it kept? Who would own it? What is its history? How might it be preserved or destroyed?

7. Describe _____ as a disease. How would it be contracted? What medicine would cure it? Who would be most likely to suffer from it? What would the chances of recovery be? What kind of specialist would treat it?

8. Describe _____ as a prepared item of food. What are the main ingredients? What types of utensils are needed to prepare it? How long does it take to cook? What type of restaurant would serve it? When would the dish be most appropriately served?

9. Describe _____ as a process. When is this process most likely to occur? What are the components of the process? What kinds of technicians are needed to make sure the process is done correctly? Can the process be improved?

10. Describe _____ as a machine. What is its major purpose? Who designed it? What is it used for? How many are needed for a business or household? Is it obsolete or state of the art?

After discussing these questions, the groups return to the main group and share their metaphors. A recorder writes down the most significant ideas for everyone. The generated list is reproduced and handed out. This exercise is thought-provoking as a culminating activity.

Advantages: The metaphor serves as a device to both explore and unify a topic. Working in this creative way places information into the students' long-term memory bank. It also effectively stimulates writing and speaking assignments. Unexpected results often occur, and the best performances in speaking and writing can result. One of my students who suffered from stuttering delivered a flawless speech by comparing a political situation to the game of baseball.

Variations:

1. The questions can be used to initiate creative or essay writing.
2. Metaphoric thinking can introduce subjects and help uncover existing attitudes and knowledge.
3. These questions can help students design speeches. Groups or individuals can brainstorm ideas for the development of topics.
4. Carry the assignment one step further by designing a game.

Assessment:

1. Groups prepare evaluation sheets for listener responses.
2. Group A evaluates Group C. Group B evaluates Group D. Then the groups exchange places. The evaluations should take some creative form. They can be puns, cartoons, skits, or an extension of the metaphor.

Projecting Exercise 5: Media Response

Objective: To view a film from the viewpoint of a character and interpret events in a variety of ways from that perspective.

Approach: Assign groups to a particular character prior to showing a film. The film is usually one that corresponds to a work of literature. Many are available and range from dramatizations of short stories, novels, and dramas to musicals of familiar stories. The film can introduce a literary work or be the culminating experience. The challenge for the students is to notice how "you" as a character react to situations and other characters. What are "your" feelings?

Students will write observations about the situations and monologues in the persona of their character. They will study the character for a performance. Show the film. If it is full length, this may take several days. Stop the film before the end of the class period to allow the character groups to share findings about their character.

When the film ends, character groups meet to share their views and to plan a presentation for the class. This presentation requires that the character groups select significant scenes, or portions of scenes, that illustrate key understandings. It may be necessary for groups to watch the film more than once. For that reason it is wise to reserve a space in the media center where groups can view the film together. If there is no such viewing room, it is often possible to arrange for the video to be set up in an empty space.

Each group presents a selected scene or scenes. To do this they may use their original monologues, dialogues, tableaus, narration, music, slides, videos, and computer-assisted programs.

Advantages: Students study a character from an actor/ producer/ director standpoint. The absorption in the role helps to extend understanding. This provides a chance to spend time on drama techniques. Knowing characters well enough to portray them and place them in situations where they must react in role demands an understanding that goes beyond a literary critique.

Variations:

1. Students can engage in improvisations for scenes with members of the character groups.

2. Students can correspond online with other characters, writing e-mail questions, responding, and creating group character analysis.

3. Groups take their performances to other classes and begin a tradition of drama exchange.

Assessment:

1. Individuals prepare character-study booklets that contain notes on the character, reactions to scenes, perceptions of other characters and problems. These writings can take the form of diaries, letters, journal entries in role. The booklets can also contain artifacts, maps, pictures, collages, sketches, costume and set designs.

2. The performance is evaluated for effort, accuracy, and significance of the observations.

Projecting Exercise 6: Issue Exploration

Objective: To devise a poetic response to an issue or problem.

Approach: Students view a series of short videos on a selected issue such as human relations, environmental concerns, race and class issues, violence, poverty, death, children's problems, or AIDS. After each video, students write short journal responses before any discussion.

Small groups then meet to explore ideas raised by the films and bring their ideas back to the whole class for discussion. When students have accumulated some information and several writings, with the assistance of the teacher, they learn how to transform one or more of these writings into free verse. The next step is to meet in the small groups to share, respond, and revise.

This process works as a springboard for writing and reading poems that address human or societal problems. Many poems speak to these concerns. "In Bed with a Book" by Mona Van Duyn, "The Century's Decline" by Wislawa Szymborska, "Hunger" by Adrienne Rich, "An Elementary Classroom in a Slum" by Stephen Spender are just a few. End this creative writing/speaking unit with a creative performance where students read their own and published poetry to the accompaniment of art, music, or dance. The goal is to convey an understanding of the issue or problem on a level beyond the denotation of words that might describe it.

Advantages: Students must attend to the details of these films and perceive meanings. Having to think about a problem and know the scope of it well enough to translate it into a poetic response, encourages students to experience knowledge on a different level.

Variations:

1. Groups of students can present their views on the issues or problems in symposiums comprised of talks and readings, followed by questions from the audience.

2. More than one issue or problem can be explored, with groups of students choosing the topic.

3. Students can videotape their performances instead of doing them in front of a live audience.

Assessment:

1. Listener responses should include a request for feedback on the impact of the message, not just the content. Listeners should note how language influences thought and feeling.

2. Evaluations by the teacher include the level of participation by all group members, the quality of the material, originality of thought, and the overall effect.

3. Students provide an analysis of the issue based on the poetic responses as well as the information received from the videos.

4. Students do a self-check of their own participation in the group and an evaluation of the effectiveness of the group process.

5. The students' creative writings (journals and poems) are evaluated by the predetermined criteria.

Conclusion

Thinking, real thinking, takes time. The kind of thinking that examines a subject in depth, probes for unexpected meanings, discovers alternative possibilities, and finds underlying flaws in apparent truths is not a hasty process. None of the above exercises are quick fixes to bring about superior thinking. They do not rely on formulae, nor are they foolproof. There is an element of trial and error in all of them because outcomes are not predetermined.

We should not surmise the process is haphazard, however. Decisions are made. Projects are completed and the results assessed. We can realize a progression in skills without accepting the notion that forms of thinking must be taught in isolation, or even in some preordered sequence. The best thinking may happen intuitively, absent a problem-solving prescription. At times, formal reasoning and structured argument may be the most fruitful approach. Our students should be aware that critical thinkers employ a number of avenues to unravel life's mysteries.

If no method of thinking is best or the only way, we must tap the mind's hidden resources through as many devices as possible. When students experiment with ideas through their own language, they have a chance to connect new information to what they already know. As human beings we are a strange combination of opposing vital forces. The need to be individuals competes with the equally strong need to belong to a social group. In a communication-based classroom we can foster both of those forces. We value language for communication in the ordinary sense of building better relationships. We also must value language in the extraordinary sense of nurturing better thinking.

The teacher's role in this process is unique. We have to develop the open, yet disciplined, attitude of scientists in pursuit of new knowledge. How we arrange our learning environment, how we monitor the events taking place there, and how we interpret the results are all subjects for careful study. The evidence we collect today becomes the basis for improving learning tomorrow. The challenge exists to raise the thinking ability for all students, regardless of their gender, ethnic, racial, or economic background.

While our goal may be idealistic, it is not impossible. Some time-honored traditions may have to change. We may have to decide it is more important to guide students through the processes of thinking than "cover" a subject. Youngsters who learn differently must have a chance to develop their skills. All learners should acquire the advantage of effective oral communication skills.

The elements of critical thinking are complex, and we omit the affective domain at our peril. Critical thinking is influenced by speaking and listening in the most profound sense. The responsibility lies in our hands. All youngsters deserve to have the best intellectual and economic opportunities the twenty-first century offers.

Appendix A

IRA/NCTE
Standards for the English Language Arts

1. Students read a wide range of print and nonprint texts to build an understanding of texts, of themselves, and of the cultures of the United States and the world; to acquire new information; to respond to the needs and demands of society and the workplace; and for personal fulfillment. Among these texts are fiction and nonfiction, classic and contemporary works.

2. Students read a wide range of literature from many periods in many genres to build an understanding of the many dimensions (e.g., philosophical, ethical, aesthetic) of human experience.

3. Students apply a wide range of strategies to comprehend, interpret, evaluate, and appreciate texts. They draw on their prior experience, their interactions with other readers and writers, their knowledge of word meaning and other texts, their word identification strategies, and their understanding of textual features (e.g., sound-letter correspondence, sentence structure, context, graphics).

4. Students adjust their use of spoken, written, and visual language (e.g., conventions, style, vocabulary) to communicate effectively with a variety of audiences and for different purposes.

5. Students employ a wide range of strategies as they write and use different writing process elements appropriately to communicate with different audiences and for different purposes.

6. Students apply knowedge of language structure, language conventions (e.g., spelling and punctuation), media techniques, figurative language, and genre to create, critique, and discuss print and nonprint texts.

7. Students conduct research on issues and interests by generating ideas and questions, and by posing problems. They gather, evaluate, and synthesize data from a variety of sources (e.g., print and nonprint texts, artifacts, people) to communicate their discoveries in ways that suit their purpose and audience.

8. Students use a variety of technological and informational resources (e.g., libraries, databases, computer networks, videos) to gather and synthesize information and to create and communicate knowledge.

9. Students develop an understanding of and respect for diversity in language use, patterns, and dialects across cultures, ethnic groups, geographic regions, and social roles.

10. Students whose first language is not English make use of their first language to develop competency in the English language arts and to develop understanding of content across the curriculum.

11. Students participate as knowledgeable, reflective, creative, and critical members of a variety of literacy communities.

12. Students use spoken, written, and visual language to accomplish their own purposes (e.g., for learning, enjoyment, persuasion, and the exchange of information).

Appendix B

National Communication Association Standards for Speaking, Listening, and Media Literacy in K–12 Education

Fundamentals of Effective Communication

Competent communicators demonstrate knowledge and understanding of

1. The relationships among the components of the communication process
2. The influence of the individual, relationship, and situation on communication
3. The role of communication in the development and maintenance of personal relationships
4. The role of communication in creating meaning, influencing thought, and making decisions

Competent communicators demonstrate the ability to

5. Demonstrate sensitivity to diversity when communicating
6. Enhance relationships and resolve conflict using appropriate and effective communication strategies
7. Evaluate communication styles, strategies, and content based on their aesthetic and functional worth
8. Show sensitivity to the ethical issues associated with communication in a democratic society

Speaking

Competent speakers demonstrate

9. Knowledge and understanding of the speaking process
10. The ability to adapt communication strategies appropriately and effectively according to the needs of the situation and setting
11. The ability to use language that clarifies, persuades, and/or inspires while respecting differences in listeners' backgrounds
12. The ability to manage or overcome communication anxiety

Listening

Competent listeners demonstrate

13. Knowledge and understanding of the listening process
14. The ability to use appropriate and effective listening skills for a given communication situation and setting
15. The ability to identify and manage barriers to listening

Media Literacy

Media literate communicators demonstrate

16. Knowledge and understanding of the ways people use media in their personal and public lives
17. Knowledge and understanding of the complex relationships among audiences and media content
18. Knowledge and understanding that media content is produced within social and cultural contexts
19. Knowledge and understanding of the commercial nature of media
20. The ability to use media to communicate to specific audiences

(*Competent Communicators: K–12 Speaking, Listening, and Media Literacy Standards and Competency Statements*. Annandale, VA: National Communication Association: 3. Copyright by the Speech Communication Association [now the National Communication Association]. 1998. Reproduced by permission of the publisher.)

Appendix C

The National Curriculum

English Key Stage 3 and 4, Programme of Study
Speaking and Listening

Pupils' abilities should be developed within an integrated programme of speaking and listening, reading and writing. Pupils should be given opportunities that interrelate the requirements of the Range, Key Skills, and Standard English and Language Study sections.

1. Range

   a) Pupils should be given opportunites to talk for a range of purposes, including:
      - explanation, description, and narration;
      - exploration and hypothesis;
      - consideration of ideas, literature, and the media;
      - argument, debate, and persuasion;
      - the development of thinking;
      - analysis.

   b) Pupils should be given opportunities to talk in a range of contexts, including those that are more formal. They should be encouraged to adapt their presentation to different audiences and to reflect on how their talk varies.

   c) Pupils should be encouraged to listen attentively, both in situations where they remain mostly silent and where they have the opportunity to respond immediately. They should be taught to distinguish features of presentation where the intention is to be explanatory, persuasive, amusing, or argumentative, and should be taught to use this knowledge when preparing and presenting their own oral work.

   d) Pupils should be given opportunities to participate in a wide range of drama activities, including role-play, and in the performance of scripted and unscripted plays. Pupils should be encouraged to develop both their communication skills and their ability to evaluate language use. In responding to drama, they should be given opportunities to consider significant features of their own and others' performances.

2. Key Skills

    a) Pupils should be given opportunities to make different types of contributions in discussion, adapting their speech to their listeners and to the activity. They should be encouraged to structure their talk clearly, judging the appropriate level of detail, and using a range of markers to aid the listener. They should be taught to use gesture and intonation appropriately. In discussions, they should be encouraged to take different views into account, sift, summarize and use salient points, cite evidence, and construct persuasive arguments. In taking different roles in group discussions, pupils should be introduced to ways of negotiating consensus or agreeing to differ. They should be given opportunities to consider their choice of words and the effectiveness of their expression.

    b) In order to develop as effective listeners, pupils should be taught to identify the major elements of what is being said and to distinguish tone, undertone, implications, and other indicators of a speaker's intentions. They should be taught to notice ambiguities, deliberate vagueness, glossing over points, use and abuse of evidence, and unsubstantiated statements. In discussion, pupils should listen and respond. They should be encouraged to make contributions that clarify and synthesize others' ideas, taking them forward and building on them to reach conclusion. Pupils should be encouraged to ask and answer questions and to modify their ideas in the light of what others say.

3. Standard English and Language Study

    a) Pupils should be taught to be fluent, accurate users of Standard English vocabulary and grammar, and to recognize its importance as the language of public communication. They should be taught to adapt their talk to suit the circumstances, and to be confident users of Standard English in formal and informal situations. In role-play and drama, the vocabulary, structures, and tone appropriate to such contexts should be explored.

    b) Pupils should be given opportunities to consider the development of English, including:
- how usage, words, and meanings change over time;
- how words and parts of words are borrowed from other languages;
- the coinage of new words and the origins of existing words;
- current influences on spoken and written language;

- attitudes to language use;
- the differences between speech and writing;
- the vocabulary and grammar of Standard English and dialectical variations.

("English Key Stage 3 and 4, Programme of Study," The National Curriculum. Copyright for the DfEE information held on NISS Services, August 20, 1996, *info@dfee.gov.uk.:1–2.* Crown copyright is reproduced with the permission of the Controller of Her Majesty's Stationery Office.)

Appendix D

Resources for Speaking and Listening Across the Curriculum

Allen, M., S. Berkowitz, S. Hunt, and A. Louden. 1999. "A Meta-analysis of the Impact of Forensics and Communication on Critical Thinking." *Communication Education* 48(1): 18–30.

Allen, R. R., S. C. Willmington, and J. Sprague. 1991. *Communication in the Secondary School: A Pedagogy.* 3d ed. Scottsdale, AZ: Gorsuch Scarisbrick.

Barnes, J. A., and A. F. Hayes. 1995. "Integration of the Language Arts and Teacher Training: An Examination of Speech Communication Instruction in the High School English Classroom." *Communication Education* 44(4): 307–20.

Berko, R. 1994. *Effective Instructional Strategies: Increasing Speaking/Listening Achievement in K–12.* Annandale, VA: Speech Communication Association.

Berko, R. M., S. P. Morreale, P. J. Cooper, and C. D. Perry. 1998. "Communication Standards and Competencies for Kindergarten Through Grade 12: The Role of the National Communication Association." *Communication Education* 47(2): 183–93.

Buckley, M. F. 1995. "Oral Language: A Curriculum Yet to Come." *English Journal* 84(1): 41–45.

Buys, W. E., T. Sill, and R. Beck. 1991. *Speaking by Doing: A Speaking-Listening Text.* 6th ed. Lincolnwood, IL: National Textbook Company.

Coakley, C. G. 1993. *Teaching Effective Listening: A Practical Guide for the High School Classroom.* Vol 1. New Orleans: Spectra.

———. 1996. *Teaching Effective Listening: A Practical Guide for the High School Classroom.* Vol 2. Sonoma, CA: Carolyn Gwynn Coakley.

Competent Communicators: K–12 Speaking, Listening, and Media Literacy Standards and Competency Statements. 1998. Annandale, VA: National Communication Association.

Cotton, E. G. 1996. *The Online Classroom: Teaching with the Internet,* 2d ed. Bloomington, IN: ERIC Clearinghouse on Reading, English, and Communication. ED 400 577.

Daly, J. A., P. O. Kreiser, and L. A. Roghar. 1994. "Question-Asking Comfort: Explorations of the Demography of Communication in the Eighth Grade Classroom." *Communication Education* 43(1): 27–41.

Daniel, A. V., ed. 1992. *Activities Integrating Oral Communication Skills for Students K–8.* Annandale, VA: Speech Communication Association.

Golub, J. 1994. *Activities for an Interactive Classroom*. Urbana, IL: National Council of Teachers of English.

Guidelines for Developing Oral Communication Curricula in Kindergarten Through Twelfth Grade. 1991. Annandale, VA: Speech Communication Association.

McCroskey, J. C., and V. P. Richmond. 1991. *Quiet Children and the Classroom Teacher*. Annandale, VA: Speech Communication Association and ERIC Clearinghouse on Reading and Communication Skills.

———. 1992. "An Instructional Communication Program for In-Service Teachers." *Communication Education* 41 (April): 215–23.

Morreale, S. P., P. M. Backlund. 1996. *Large Scale Assessment of Oral Communication: K–12 and Higher Education*. 2d ed. Annandale, VA: Speech Communication Association.

National Forensic League, P.O. Box 38, Ripon, WI 54971–0038.

O'Keefe, V. P. 1992. "Review Essay: Intermediate and Secondary Level Textbooks in Speech Communication." *Communication Education* 41(4): 440–51.

———. 1995. *Speaking to Think/Thinking to Speak: The Importance of Talk in the Learning Process*. Portsmouth, NH: Heinemann–Boynton/Cook.

Rancer, A. S., V. Whitecap, R. L. Kosberg, and T. A. Avtgis. 1997. "Training in Argumentativeness: Testing the Efficacy of a Communication Training Program to Increase Argumentativeness and Argumentative Behavior." *Communication Education* 46(4): 273–86.

Rubin, R., S. A. Welch, and R. Buerkel. 1995. "Performance-Based Assessment of High School Speech Instruction." *Communication Education* 44(1): 30–39.

Witkin, B. R., M. L. Lovern, and S. W. Lundsteen. 1996. "Oral Communication in the English Language Arts Curriculum." *Communication Education* 45(1): 40–58.

References

Adler, M. J. 1982. *The Paideia Proposal: An Educational Manifesto.* New York: Macmillan.

The Arkansas English Language Arts and Mathematics Curriculum Frameworks. 1993. Arkansas Department of Education.

"Average Score on AP Tests High Enough to Earn Credits, Placement." 1996. *Virginia Journal of Education* (November): 5.

Barnes, D. 1976. *From Communication to Curriculum.* New York: Penguin Books.

Beyer, B. K. 1991. "What Philosophy Offers to the Teaching of Thinking." In *Developing Minds: A Resource Book for Teaching Thinking,* rev. ed., vol. 1, ed. A. L. Costa, 72–76. Alexandria, VA: Association for Supervision and Curriculum Development.

Bloom, B. S., ed. 1979. *Taxonomy of Educational Objectives: Book 1 Cognitive Domain.* London: Longman.

Bloom, B. S., D. R. Krathwohl, and B. B. Masia. 1973. *Taxonomy of Educational Objectives: Book 2 Affective Domain.* London: Longman.

Boyer, E. L. 1983. *High School: A Report on Secondary Education in America.* New York: Harper & Row.

Brilhart, J. K., and G. J. Galanes. 1989. *Effective Group Discussion.* Cambridge, MA: Harvard University Press.

Britton, J. N. 1980. *Language and Learning.* London: Penguin Books.

———. 1982a. "Poetry and Our Pattern of Culture." In *Prospect and Retrospect: Selected Essays of James Britton,* ed. G. M. Pradl, 24–31. Montclair, NJ: Boynton/Cook.

———. 1982b. "The Role of Fantasy." In *Prospect and Retrospect: Selected Essays of James Britton,* ed. G. M. Pradl, 38–45. Montclair, NJ: Boynton/Cook.

———. 1982c. "Shaping at the Point of Utterance." In *Prospect and Retrospect: Selected Essays of James Britton,* ed. G. M. Pradl, 139–45. Montclair, NJ: Boynton/Cook.

———. 1982d. "Words and the Imagination." In *Prospect and Retrospect: Selected Essays of James Britton,* ed. G. M. Pradl, 20–31. Montclair, NJ: Boynton/Cook.

Bruner, J. S. 1977. *The Process of Education.* Cambridge, MA: Harvard University Press.

Caine, R. N., and G. Caine. 1991. *Teaching and the Human Brain.* Alexandria, VA: Association for Supervision and Curriculum Development.

Chaffee, J. 1994. *Thinking Critically,* 4th ed. Boston: Houghton Mifflin.

Competent Communicators: K–12 Speaking, Listening, and Media Literacy Standards and Competency Statements. 1998. Annandale, VA: National Communication Association.

Cooper, P. J. 1995. *Speech Communication for the Classroom Teacher.* Scottsdale, AZ: Gorsuch Scarisbrick.

Cooperative Learning and the Gifted. 1998. National Research Center on the Gifted and Talented, Project ID 8103:1.

Dewey, J. E. 1910. *How We Think.* Boston: D. C. Heath.

Dickinson, E. 1981. "The Brain Is Wider Than the Sky." In *The Norton Introduction to Literature,* 3d ed., ed. C. E. Bain, J. Beaty, and J. P. Hunter, 845. New York: W. W. Norton.

Dillon, J. T. 1995. *Using Discussion in Classrooms.* Buckingham, Great Britain: Open University Press.

Framework for English Language Arts, Preliminary Draft. 1994. New York State Education Department.

Freeman, J. 1995. "What's Right with Schools." *ERIC Digest* 93 (February). ED78665.

Fryar, M., D. A. Thomas, and L. Goodnight. 1989. *Basic Debate.* 3d ed. Skokie, IL: National Textbook Company.

Gardner, H. 1991. *The Unschooled Mind.* New York: Basic Books.

Gibbs, R. W. 1995. *The Poetics of Mind: Figurative Thought, Language, and Understanding.* Cambridge: Cambridge University Press.

Good, T. L., and J. E. Brophy. 1991. *Looking into Classrooms,* 5th ed. New York: HarperCollins.

Gordon, W. J. J. 1961. *Synectics: The Development of Creative Capacity.* New York: Harper & Row.

Hall, B. I., S. P. Morreale, and J. L. Gaudino. 1999. "A Survey of the Status of Oral Communication in the K–12 Public Educational System in the United States." *Communication Education* 43(2): 139–48.

Hiraoka, L. 1998. "The International Test Scores Are In . . ." *NEA Today* (May): 19.

How Schools Shortchange Girls: A Study of Major Findings on Girls and Education. 1992. Washington, D.C.: American Association of University Women Educational Foundation and National Education Association.

Jensen, E. 1998. *Teaching with the Brain in Mind.* Alexandria, VA: Association for Supervision and Curriculum Development.

Johnson, S. D. 1994. "A National Assessment of Secondary School Principals' Perception of Teaching-Effectiveness Criteria." *Communication Education* 43(1): 1–16.

Kelly, G. A. 1963. *A Theory of Personality: The Psychology of Personal Constructs.* New York: W. W. Norton.

Lessing, D. 1976. "The Witness." In *The Habit of Loving*, 122–36. New York: New American Library.

Lewis, C. C., E. Schaps, M. S. Watson. 1996. "The Caring Classroom's Academic Edge." *Educational Leadership* 54(1): 16–21.

Marzano, R. J. 1992. *A Different Kind of Classroom: Teaching with Dimensions of Learning.* Alexandria, VA: Association for Supervision and Curriculum Development.

Marzano, R. J., D. Pickering, J. McTighe. 1993. *Assessing Student Outcomes: Performance Assessment Using the Dimensions of Learning Model.* Alexandria, VA: Association for Supervison and Curriculum Development.

McClellan, M. 1994. "Why Blame Schools?" *Research Bulletin* 12. (March). Phi Delta Kappa, Center for Evaluation.

McCreesh, J. 1977. "Children's Ideas of Horror and Tragedy." In *The Cool Web: The Patterns of Children's Reading*, ed. M. Meek, A. Warlow, and G. Barton, 112–20. London: Bodley Head.

McCroskey, J. C., and V. P. Richmond. 1991. *Quiet Children and the Classroom Teacher.* Bloomington, IN: ERIC, and Annandale, VA: Speech Communication Association.

McCutcheon, R., J. Schaffer, J. R. Wycoff. 1994. *Communication Matters.* Minneapolis/St. Paul: West.

McPeck, J. E. 1981. *Critical Thinking and Education.* Oxford: Martin Robinson.

"Meeting Goal 3: How Well Are We Doing?" 1992. *Education Research Report* (October): 1–4.

Meyers, C. 1986. *Teaching Students to Think Critically.* San Francisco: Jossey-Bass.

Moffett, J. 1968. *Teaching the Universe of Discourse.* Boston: Houghton Mifflin.

National Forensic League. 1990. "Table of Most Frequently Used Parliamentary Motions." In *Student Congress Manual*, SCM-5. Ripon, WI: National Forensic League.

O'Keefe, V. 1988. "Student Discourse in a Secondary English Class: A Descriptive Case Study of the Connections Between Speaking and Writing Activities and Understanding of a Literary Text." In *Dissertation Abstracts International.* Ann Arbor, MI: University Microfilms, No. 8825256.

———. 1995. *Speaking to Think, Thinking to Speak.* Portsmouth, NH: Heinemann–Boynton/Cook.

Patrick, J. J. 1993. "Achievement of Goal Three of the Six National Education Goals." *ERIC Digest* (May).

Perkins, D. 1992. *Smart Schools: From Training Memories to Training Minds.* New York: Free Press.

Piaget, J., and B. Inhelder. 1979. *The Psychology of the Child.* London: Redwood Burn, Trowbridge and Esher.

Research Overview. 1998. Centre for the Study of Learning and Performance. Montreal: CSLP Research Activities.

Resnick, L. B., and L. E. Klopfer. 1989. "Toward the Thinking Curriculum: An Overview." In *Toward the Thinking Curriculum: Current Cognitive Research,* ed. L. B. Resnick and L. E. Klopfer, 1–18. Alexandria, VA: Association for Supervision and Curriculum Development.

Riley, R. W. 1995. "The State of American Education." *Virginia Journal of Education* (April): 7–12.

"School Evaluation Matters: What Is School Evaluation?" 1998. UK, OFSTED, London: Crown.

Smagorinsky, P. 1996. *Standards in Practice Grades 9–12.* Urbana, IL: National Council of Teachers of English.

Smith, F. 1990. *To Think.* New York and London: Teachers College Press.

Speech Communication Association. 1989. *Pathways to Careers in Communication.* Annandale, VA: Speech Communication Association.

Standards for the English Language Arts. 1996. Urbana, IL: National Council of Teachers of English and International Reading Association.

Standards of Learning for Virginia Public Schools. 1995. Richmond, VA: Board of Education, Commonwealth of Virginia.

Subjects and Standards: Issues for School Development Arising from OFSTED Inspection Findings 1994–5, Key Stages 3 & 4 and Post-16. 1996. London: HMSO.

Sylvester, R. 1995. *A Celebration of Neurons.* Alexandria, VA: Association for Supervision and Curriculum Development.

Talk Workshop Group. 1982. *Becoming Our Own Experts: Studies in Language and Learning Made by the Talk Workshop Group at Vauxhall Manor School, 1974–79.* London: Talk Workshop Group.

Tama, M. C. 1989. "Critical Thinking: Promoting It in the Classroom." *ERIC Digest* (June).

Teacher Handbook Communication Skills K–12. 1992. Raleigh, NC: North Carolina Department of Public Instruction.

Tough, J. 1979. *The Development of Meaning: A Study of Children's Use of Language.* New York: John Wiley & Sons.

————. 1980. *Talking and Learning.* London: Ward Lock Educational.

Vladero, D. 1999. "Higher Standards." *U.S. News and World Report* 126(2): 52–55.

Vygotsky, L. S. 1978. *Mind in Society: The Development of Higher Psychological Processes.* Cambridge, MA: Harvard University Press.

Winnicott, D. W. 1971. *Playing and Reality.* New York: Basic Books.

"Within Reach?" 1998. *Virginia Journal of Education* (February): 7–10.

Wolff, F. I., N. C. Marsnick, W. S. Tacey, and R. G. Nichols. 1983. *Perceptive Listening.* New York: Holt, Rinehart, and Winston.

Wolvin, A., and C. G. Coakley. 1992. *Listening,* 4th ed. Dubuque, IA: Wm. C. Brown.

Index